Praise for
Around the Bible in 80 Days

"There are so many airy-fairy, otherworldly devotionals that orient us away from the concrete realities of God's good creation. Finally, here we have a brilliant daily devotional that affirms the goodness of creation, clarifies the forward thrust of the biblical story as God's purpose to redeem the world, and celebrates the new creation achieved through the coming of Jesus the Messiah! It is my hope that *Around the Bible in 80 Days* will be widely read in the church—and beyond. It will not only give encouragement for Christians who desire holistic meditations on Scripture, it may introduce others to a marvelous vision of reality they never knew existed."

—**J. Richard Middleton,** Professor of Biblical Worldview and Exegesis, Northeastern Seminary at Roberts Wesleyan College, Boston, MA

"John Mark Hicks's teaching on and, more importantly, modeling of a theological reading of Scripture is essential for our time, especially in the Restoration Movement. I have found his work, to which I have returned again and again, as useful and compelling for churches in West Africa as it is for churches in the Bible Belt."

—**Nathan Bills,** Lecturer and Ag Head of the Department of Theology, Heritage Christian College, Accra, Ghana

"In this broken world, many live their lives in suffering and injustice as though they are stuck in a sea storm they cannot escape. Human beings who are created with wonderful potential have lost their identity and purpose. Hicks offers an eighty-day journey through the Bible where readers may rediscover their identity through a narration of the biblical drama of how God pursues humanity within the creation. This true story invites people to participate in his mission of transformation and restoration. That invitation extends to each of us."

—**Ronald Quilaton,** Founder of 8:18 Missions International, Cebu City, Philippines

"What a wonderful book! A vast amount of scholarship distilled into eighty concise, accessible, and engaging essays. For years I've been hoping John Mark would write such a book, because he is an excellent thinker and teacher who has been refining this material with great care and attention. Even more, John Mark's love for Jesus and the church is apparent on every page as he invites readers to become full participants in the great theodrama revealed in Scripture."

—**Josh Strahan,** Associate Professor of Bible, Lipscomb University

"Hicks serves as a wise guide on a journey through the biblical story. He both points out what is familiar and reminds us why it matters and, perhaps, opens our eyes to things we haven't noticed before. These eighty devotionals join Scripture, theology, and prayer in a most helpful and edifying way as we move through the story of God in Scripture from creation to New Creation."

—**Phillip Camp,** Professor of Bible, Hazelip School of Theology, Lipscomb University

"In *Around the Bible in 80 Days*, John Mark Hicks combines his usual sound theological teaching with an opportunity for us to understand and worship God more fully while at the same time helping the 'self' to mature with each chapter. The classic combination of a biblical text, a reader-oriented interpretation, a space for thoughtful reflection, and an adoration in prayer gives well-needed orientation for living out our human vocation every day."

—**Dr. Markus Zobec,** Lead Pastor, Paulus-Gemeinde Bremen, Germany

"In eighty short essays, John Mark Hicks offers us a daily opportunity to experience the grand sweep of the story of God's creation and re-creation of all things. Most importantly, Hicks shows the reader how the love and grace of God saturate this story. This love invites us, who are created in God's image, to participate in God's redemptive work as we anticipate the fulfillment of all things in loving communion—in Christ and through the Holy Spirit—between God and all creation. It's breathtaking, so it takes a while to take it in. Take eighty days."

—**Dr. Carisse Mickey Berryhill,** Special Assistant to the Dean for Strategic Initiatives, Brown Library, Abilene Christian University

"In eighty days, John Mark Hicks takes us on a journey through the greatest story ever told. The text, reflection, meditation, and prayer combine to form an understanding of God and his world around us that is truly life changing. Understanding the theodrama has transformed my life and ministry, and I'm confident the Lord will use this book to transform the lives and hearts of his Church."

—**Matthew Stidham,** Lead Minister, Countryside Christian Church, Nixa, Missouri

"Applying his approach to theological interpretation, structuring it around the design and destiny of creation, and connecting all the basic narratives of the Bible, John Mark Hicks has created a masterpiece among his writings. I pray many people will read this book, be drawn near to God, and be enlightened by the Spirit to live as disciples of the Lord Jesus and tell the world about God's saving story."

—**Eduardo "Bro. Jhun" Ma Jr.,** Minister, Tuao Church of Christ, Tuao Cagayan Valley, Philippines

"Walking through the theodrama of God, John Mark Hicks takes us through the history of God with the world in eighty days from creation to new creation. Everyone across the world will benefit from his introduction to the drama of God's coming to dwell with humanity within the creation. Watching this drama unfold, we are all drawn closer to God's footstool, and this enhances our hope to dwell with God eternally along with all the followers of King Jesus."

—**P. Anil Kumar,** Evangelist, Chilakaluripet, India

"This book is a refreshing read of the story of scripture. Avoiding the traps of centuries of scholarly and even dogmatic debate, the work allows us to actually enjoy the story. The reader should not think the book is bereft of meaty theological content. Such content is there, but it appears in such a way as to be easily digestible and creatively thoughtful. Each session provides a provocative question for discussion as well as a devotional thought. Throughout the reading, I found compelling reasons to shout *AMEN*!"

—**Dr. Michael A. Brown,** Senior Minister, Westview Church of Christ, Huntsville, AL

"*Around the Bible in 80 Days* is a much-needed resource that is sure to enrich and deepen your knowledge and faith. It is unusual to see such rich biblical teaching organized and communicated in a way that will touch both the mind and the heart. This is a book people will be sure to come back to year after year to reconnect with these truths, questions, and prayers!"

—**Matt Dabbs,** Church Planter, Auburn, Alabama; Editor of Wineskins.org

"In this small but remarkable book, Hicks has given a gift to thoughtful Christians—a collection of substantive devotions rooted in the best of biblical scholarship. But the best part is the fact that these devotions are not stand-alone, disconnected reflections. Rather, they tell a cohesive story, reminding us that the Bible is not a collection of atomized facts but a grand and majestic narrative with Jesus at the center."

—**Richard T. Hughes,** Author, *Reviving the Ancient Faith: The Story of Churches of Christ in America*

"In a world of competing voices and narratives, there is only one story that has the capacity to both transform and redeem. John Mark Hicks invites us to find ourselves in the story of God in a way that encourages us to grow deeper in our faith and see God's grand design for us. I'm looking forward to walking with my congregation through this exceptional resource."

—**Chris Harrell,** Lead Minister, Compass Church, Jonesboro, Arkansas

AROUND THE BIBLE IN 80 DAYS

AROUND THE BIBLE IN 80 DAYS

JOHN MARK HICKS

AROUND THE BIBLE IN 80 DAYS

The Story of God from Creation to New Creation

ISBN 978-1-68426-461-2

Printed in the United States of America

LIBRARY OF CONGRESS CATALOGING-IN-PUBLICATION DATA
Names: Hicks, John Mark, author.
Title: Around the Bible in eighty days : the story of God from creation to new creation / John Mark Hicks.
Description: Abilene, Texas : Leafwood Publishers, 2022.
Identifiers: LCCN 2021036941 | ISBN 9781684264612 (paperback)
Subjects: LCSH: Bible—Criticism, interpretation, etc.
Classification: LCC BS511.3 .H525 2022 | DDC 220.07—dc23
LC record available at https://lccn.loc.gov/2021036941

Cover design by Bruce Gore
Interior text design by Sandy Armstrong, Strong Design

Leafwood Publishers is an imprint of Abilene Christian University Press
ACU Box 29138
Abilene, Texas 79699

1-877-816-4455
www.leafwoodpublishers.com

25 26 27 28 29 30 / 7 6 5 4 3

Dedicatory Prayer

May God, through the grace of the Lord Jesus and the power of the Holy Spirit, use this offering not only as a reflection on the meaning and significance of God's story but also as an invitation to participate in it.

CONTENTS

PREFACE A Theodrama 15

DAY 1 The Five Acts of the Theodrama 19

ACT ONE
CREATION

DAY 2 Why Did God Create the World? 25

DAY 3 God Builds a House 27

DAY 4 From "Empty and Void" to "Very Good" 29

DAY 5 Human Identity: The Image of God 31

DAY 6 The Human Vocation: Fill the Earth 34

DAY 7 The Human Vocation: Subdue the Earth 37

DAY 8 The Human Vocation: Rule the Earth 39

DAY 9 Two Trees: A Wisdom Story 42

DAY 10 Humanity Tumbled: A Disordered Earth 45

DAY 11 Humanity Tumbled: Violence Enters the World 48

DAY 12 Humanity Tumbled: Violence Encompasses the Earth 51

DAY 13 Humanity Degenerated: An Alternative Story 54

ACT TWO
ISRAEL

DAY 14 The Promise to Abraham 59

DAY 15 Israel as New Humanity 61

DAY 16 Israel as a Royal Priest among the Nations 64

DAY 17 God Dwells with Israel 66

DAY 18 Israel Inherits a Land 69

DAY 19 Israel Wants a New King 72
DAY 20 God's Gift to Israel 75
DAY 21 God's Torah: A Path to Life 77
DAY 22 The Oracles of God 80
DAY 23 The Witness of History 82
DAY 24 The Hymns and Prayers of Israel 84
DAY 25 Wisdom and Folly 87
DAY 26 Living in Chaos 89
DAY 27 The Prophet Amos Calls for Justice and Hope 92
DAY 28 The Prophets Call for Justice 95
DAY 29 The Prophets Envision a New Day 98

ACT THREE
MESSIAH

DAY 30 God Sends the Son and the Spirit 103
DAY 31 God Becomes a Human Being 106
DAY 32 Why Did God Become Human? 108
DAY 33 The Messiah Is Immersed with Israel 111
DAY 34 The Messiah Goes into the Wilderness with Israel 114
DAY 35 The Messiah Begins His Ministry 116
DAY 36 The Messiah Ministers to Israel 119
DAY 37 Seeking First the Kingdom of God and Its Righteousness 121
DAY 38 Pledging Allegiance to the Messiah's Kingdom 123
DAY 39 Did Jesus Preach the Gospel? 126
DAY 40 The Messiah Confronts the Reign of Satan 129
DAY 41 The Messiah Begins the Journey to the Cross 132
DAY 42 God Gives the Messiah Hope 135
DAY 43 The Messiah Is a Suffering Servant 138
DAY 44 The Messiah Comes to the Temple 141

DAY 45 The Messiah Establishes Kingdom Priorities 144
DAY 46 The Messiah Serves the Table 147
DAY 47 The Messiah Agonizes over Doing the Will of God 150
DAY 48 The Messiah Is Crucified 153
DAY 49 The Messiah on the Cross 156
DAY 50 The Messiah Is Abandoned 159
DAY 51 The Messiah Is Vindicated 162
DAY 52 At the Table with the Messiah on Resurrection Sunday 165
DAY 53 The Messiah Commissions His Disciples 168
DAY 54 The Messiah Is Enthroned as Lord 171
DAY 55 New Creation Inaugurated 174

ACT FOUR
CHURCH

DAY 56 The Renewal of Israel 179
DAY 57 The Pouring Out of the Spirit 182
DAY 58 The Invitation into Community: Baptism 185
DAY 59 The Formation of Community: Assembly 188
DAY 60 The Formation of Community: The Teaching of the Apostles 191
DAY 61 The Formation of Community: The Table of the Lord 194
DAY 62 The Formation of Community: Fellowship 197
DAY 63 The Formation of Community: Prayer 200
DAY 64 The Formation of Community: Leadership 203
DAY 65 Missional Mandate: Fill the Earth 206
DAY 66 Missional Mandate: Subdue the Powers 209
DAY 67 Missional Mandate: Shepherd the Creation 212
DAY 68 Life in the Spirit: Communion with God 215
DAY 69 Life in the Spirit: Transformation 217
DAY 70 Life in the Spirit: Gifts 219

ACT FIVE
NEW CREATION

DAY 71	Already, but Not Yet	225
DAY 72	Perfected through Suffering	228
DAY 73	Life in the Spirit: Lament	230
DAY 74	Life in the Spirit: Waiting in Hope	233
DAY 75	The Resurrection of Jesus	236
DAY 76	The Resurrection of Humanity	239
DAY 77	The Resurrection of Creation	242
DAY 78	Divine Judgment	245
DAY 79	New Heaven and New Earth: Communal Life	248
DAY 80	A New Garden: Renewed Identity and Vocation	251

PREFACE

A THEODRAMA

Around the Bible in 80 Days tells the big-picture story of God. It is a *theodrama*, a word I use throughout this book to describe the story or drama of God revealed in the Bible. This theological word is not of my own creation. *Theo* means God, and *drama* refers to a plot or narrative. A theodrama, therefore, is the story of God's creative and redemptive acts within history as described by the Bible. *Theodrama* is the word that encapsulates the dramatic plot at the heart of the biblical narrative. God is its main actor.

At the same time, my telling of the theodrama in eighty days is not a rehearsal of historical facts, people, or events. Though those details are neither ignored nor dismissed, my retelling reflects on the meaning and significance of different movements or acts within the dramatic plot of Scripture. My intent is to identify, highlight, and understand the key moves within the drama so we might not only know the basic plot itself but also explore its depth and meaning and, hopefully, find ourselves in the story in ways that enable us to participate in God's mission, which is central to the theodrama itself.

In general, I have stayed with the story most, if not all, Christians confess. I have attempted, with a few exceptions, to stay away from controversial issues, which are typically secondary or tertiary concerns. I intend an undenominational or nonsectarian retelling of God's story. I am probably not as successful as I want to be, however. Nevertheless, I want to tell the story of God in the Bible in a way that is not only *accessible* to all and *enriches* all but that also, hopefully, *unites* all. My intent is to tell the story all Christians, in substance, confess, while acknowledging that Christians may also see different nuances in certain aspects.

In eighty brief sections, running around 450 to 650 words each, I attempt to identify, explain, and share the fundamental arc of the biblical plot. Each section begins with a primary biblical text, retells one aspect of the story, provides a single question for meditation or reflection, and offers a brief prayer.

The story I tell through these theological snippets is essentially what I have taught, in one form or another, over the past course of my forty-year career in academia. In fact, several former students, in the endorsements that preface this book, testify to the congruity and its impact on their own lives and ministries. The story appears here in the form of mediations that both instruct and invite. I hope they have some sense of depth while, at the same time, maintaining clarity and practical significance.

How might this material be used? At a personal level, one could read one section every day over three months. In this way, it serves as a resource for personal growth and theological maturation. I would hope one could spend several minutes reading, several minutes reflecting, and several minutes praying. Ten minutes a day would introduce the theological world of the Bible for the sake of encounter with God and formation into the image of God.

At a communal level, a group—whether a small home gathering, a church Bible class, or a congregation listening to a sermon series—could use the material to walk through the story of the Bible and reflect on its meaning together. It could serve as a means of communal discernment and mutual understanding as a community seeks to live within the story of God and participate in God's mission.

Either way, my prayer is that this book will provide some access to the story of God and its depth in ways that are both helpful and transformative and that deepen the understanding of the theodrama.

Seventy-four of the eighty days first appeared on the YouTube and podcast channels of Wineskins.org. Matt Dabbs and Matthew Darwin Stidham managed the production and publication of each of the original seventy-four videos. They are still available on YouTube as a resource. While the videos are generally the same, there are some corrections, additions, and expansions within the present book that are not in the videos or podcasts. For example, the videos do not contain an opening Scripture text, a question, or a prayer. I am deeply grateful for Matt and Matthew's work. I could not have done it without them, and this book would not be what it is without them, though I am responsible for all its errors.

May God bless this offering to the church and to God seekers as a way of hearing the story of God, who came to us in Jesus by the power of the Holy Spirit. May God bless you, the reader, as you study, meditate, and pray your way through the story of God.

Peace,
John Mark Hicks
October 2021

THE FIVE ACTS OF THE THEODRAMA

TEXT: ROMANS 16:25–27

Now to God who is able to strengthen you according to my gospel and the proclamation of Jesus Christ, according to the revelation of the mystery that was kept secret for long ages but is now disclosed, and through the prophetic writings is made known to all the Gentiles, according to the command of the eternal God, to bring about the obedience of faith—to the only wise God, through Jesus Christ, to whom be the glory forever! Amen.

The Bible tells the story of God. There are many threads within that story and many rabbit trails one might pursue, but there is one overarching plot to the drama. There is, in essence, one story in five acts.

Act One—Creation
Act Two—Israel
Act Three—Messiah
Act Four—Church
Act Five—New Creation

This story has an arc that begins with creation and moves to new creation, the goal of the drama. The arc has a climax, but the climax is found in the middle. That climax is Jesus the Messiah, who is God in the flesh. The same one who was present at the beginning and through whom God created all things is also the same one God raised from the dead as the beginning of new creation. The first and final acts of the drama are performed in the person of Jesus. He, then, is the pinnacle of the arc, the one in whom both the beginning and the end find their meaning.

Between creation and Jesus lies the story of Abraham's descendants, Israel. They are the people of God whom God led into a new Eden, but they did not embrace God's mission. God invested the hope of the nations in Israel, but they did not pursue this hope. Nevertheless, God pursued them and accomplished that hope in Jesus the Messiah.

Jesus, the instrument of God's creative work in the beginning and now the reality of new creation at the right hand of God, descended from Abraham. Jesus was a Jew, and through him, God chose to bless and give hope to all nations. Jesus invites the nations into the community of Israel.

The fourth act is the church, which is the renewal of Israel's identity and vocation in the world. Moreover, it is the renewal of human identity and vocation. God recreates humanity in order to give the world hope. Through the church, God will bless all nations.

This divine drama, which has five acts, has a beginning, a goal, and a climax. Creation is the beginning, the first act of God. New creation, the new heaven and the new Earth, is the goal, the fifth act of God. Jesus the Messiah is the climax in whom all things are fulfilled, which is the story's third act. Between the first and third acts and between the third and fifth acts, God creates community. The second act is the story of Israel, and the fourth act is the story of the church that is renewed Israel, by which God invites all peoples into the life of Israel.

These are the five acts. I call them a theodrama because, taken together, they are God's story. The theodrama is the story of God's work, God's acts. God creates a good world, God elects Israel as a people for the sake of the nations, God becomes human for our salvation, God calls the nations into the life of Israel in the church, and God renews the creation.

In the coming pages, I will retell this story. Through the theodrama, God invites us to make it our own and participate in the life and mission of God—the one who created us, loves us, and redeems us.

QUESTION: How does it change your reading of the Bible to ask what God is doing rather than first asking what we are required to do in response to the story?

PRAYER: *God, open our eyes to see what you have done in the world for the sake of the world and what you are now doing to bring the world to the goal you intend for it.*

ACT ONE

CREATION

WHY DID GOD CREATE THE WORLD?

TEXT: JOHN 17:24–26

[Jesus prayed]: "Father, I desire that those also, whom you have given me, may be with me where I am, to see my glory, which you have given me because you loved me before the foundation of the world.

Righteous Father, the world does not know you, but I know you; and these know that you have sent me. I made your name known to them, and I will make it known, so that the love with which you have loved me may be in them, and I in them."

Why did God create the world? This question stretches across all age groups, from toddlers to graduate students. To be sure, it is precarious, even presumptive, to answer. We cannot get into God's head and identify motives. However, the theodrama does not leave us clueless about God's purpose and intent. But before we enter the world of the drama, let's consider a few thoughts.

On one hand, some suggest God was needy. In other words, maybe there was a hole in God's psyche. Perhaps God was lonely or needed companionship—a playmate, or worse, someone to control. I remember my daughter, for example, wanted my wife and me to have another child because she wanted someone to boss around. In effect, this sort of God is codependent, a God who needs the divine ego stroked or a deficiency filled. In this scenario, creation arises out of self-interest rather than being a gracious gift.

On the other hand, some suggest God acted arbitrarily. God had no reason to create. It was a bare assertion of sovereign power or ego. Sometimes people worship God simply because God is powerful. In that case, God may be worshiped but not adored because terror drives that worship.

Reading the whole story, from beginning to end, suggests an answer to the question. While creation was the first act of God, we learn something about God's intent by reading the rest of the story.

Christians confess that God is Father, Son, and Holy Spirit. God is not lonely. Rather, God enjoys a communion of love within the triune community. God does not need someone to love because, as Jesus prayed, the Father already loved the Son and the Son already loved the Father, even before the creation of the world.

Further, the purpose of redemption suggests the purpose of creation. Jesus prayed that his disciples would come to know God so that the love with which God loves the Son might be in them. In other words, God acts, whether in creation or redemption, to include us within the orbit of God's own communal love. God created a people to share God's own loving communion, a community that predates creation itself.

Perhaps an analogy might help. Why do we have children? There is no economic benefit, and it does not relieve family stress. However, in the best of circumstances, we have children because we want to share our love with them. We want to include others in the orbit of the family's love. We love and, therefore, we choose to create.

In a similar way, God does not create because God is lonely or needy. God creates to include others in the communion of God's own loving family. God loves, and God chooses to create.

QUESTION: In what way does God's love move God to create? How do you understand that?

PRAYER: *God of love, thank you for creating us and drawing us into your circle of love; pour your love into our hearts that we might love others like you love us.*

GOD BUILDS A HOUSE

TEXT: ISAIAH 66:1–2

Thus says the L*ORD*:
Heaven is my throne
and the earth is my footstool;
what is the house that you would build for me,
and what is my resting place?
All these things my hand has made,
and so all these things are mine,
says the L*ORD*.
But this is the one to whom I will look,
to the humble and contrite in spirit,
who trembles at my word.

When Israel agonized over what sort of house or temple they should build for God, God clarified something for them: "Thus says the Lord: Heaven is my throne, and the earth is my footstool."

The God of Israel announced some fundamental truths about creation. It is the house God built, it belongs to God, and God lives in it.

The divine hand made everything. This echoes Genesis 2, where it says that God rested from all that God had made. Everything between Genesis 1:1 and God's rest in Genesis 2 is the object of God's creating and making. Everything in the universe—including the cosmos itself—is the product of God's loving power. Whatever began to exist, God made it.

Moreover, God is enthroned within the heavens and the Earth. The "heavens" do not refer to some celestial divine sanctuary beyond the glimpse of the Hubble Telescope or to a dwelling place outside the cosmos. God did not construct a house out of brick and mortar but out of Earth and sky. The sky is God's throne, and the Earth is God's footstool. The cosmos is God's palace or temple, a cathedral of God's own making. It is God's house.

God dwells in that house. It is the place where God came to rest. This is temple language, as we know from Israel's history. When God came to dwell in the temple in Israel, it was called God's resting place (Ps. 132:14). The temple is where God dwells, and creation is God's temple. When I say God rested within the temple, I do not mean God became a couch potato or a passive observer. Instead, God dwells within the creation in order to enjoy it and share life with it.

While God was graciously present in the earthly temple in Jerusalem, God does not dwell in houses made by human hands because God dwells within the cosmos itself. God is so present in the creation that every breath is the movement of God's Spirit and every breath is communion with God. Though, as Creator, God is transcendent to the creation and is not dependent upon it, God is nevertheless graciously and immanently present within the creation to sustain life and commune with and enjoy it. God loves the creation.

Perhaps we should remember that we live in God's house and, therefore, we should treat the creation with respect and care. At the same time, God invites us to commune with the divine through the creation and revel in its joy and beauty.

Perhaps God is like an Airbnb owner who says, "Enjoy my resting place, but don't trash it." The cosmos is God's temple, so let us enjoy it with reverence and respect.

QUESTION: When we recognize creation as a cathedral of praise, in what ways does this open our eyes to see God in creation and invite our response?

PRAYER: *God, maker of heaven and Earth, we praise your great love and power!*

FROM "EMPTY AND VOID" TO "VERY GOOD"

TEXT: GENESIS 1:1–2, 31

In the beginning when God created the heavens and the earth, the earth was a formless void and darkness covered the face of the deep, while [the Spirit of God] swept over the face of the waters. . . . God saw everything that he had made, and indeed, it was very good. And there was evening and there was morning, the sixth day.

The first line of the Bible is a bold confession. "In the beginning God created the heavens and the earth" (Gen. 1:1 NIV).

The Earth began, however, as an uninhabitable mess. The Earth was a chaotic void, and darkness covered the face of the deep, as the Spirit of God hovered over the face of the waters.

At first, God created a mess. This is no moral judgment; God does not create evil. Rather, the mess was unordered, lacked arrangement, and was unsuitable for life. It was empty, void of all life, and characterized by darkness and the waters, which were terrifying images to ancient peoples.

Though the darkness and the waters covered the Earth in the beginning, God was not absent but present. The Spirit of God, who is the giver of life, hovered over the waters like a mother bird over her nest. The Spirit moved over this chaos in order to bless and pour life into it.

God created space for life by introducing the light of divine presence, by separating the sky from the waters, and by separating land from the waters. God ordered the mess so that there was light, a sky above the

Earth, and dry land upon it. God created habitable space where life might flourish. The Spirit of God, the giver of life, ordered the chaos.

God then filled the space. God filled the sky with luminaries. The Sun lit up the day, and the Moon and stars illuminated the night. God filled the waters with life, and God filled the land with creatures, including human beings.

God created the original chaotic mess, and then God formed, ordered, and crafted it into something good, very good.

God is a royal architect and artisan. God commanded, and it happened. The Word of God accomplished whatever God intended. God erected a new structure, a cosmic temple, and filled it with life and provided it with everything that makes life possible. God weaved the cosmos in such a way that it is a diverse, vibrant, and beautiful place. What God erected and weaved was good. God provided a space where life could flourish.

Good, however, does not mean complete or even perfect or ideal. God wanted the cosmos to grow and progress. New species would emerge, and humans would have children, fill the Earth, and develop multiple cultures. The creation is dynamic rather than static. Change is built into the fabric of the universe, and that, too, is good.

The creation is good, and God is not yet done with it. When God came to rest within this cosmic temple, God invited human beings to participate in the work to come. Though God finished creating the space and filling it, God was not yet done with what the creation was yet to become. The creation had a future, and that is the rest of the story.

QUESTION: When God finished creating in Genesis 1, in what ways was the creation still incomplete, or what did God intend for the future of the creation?

PRAYER: *Creator God, we give you thanks for this good creation, and with you we enjoy its beauty and diversity.*

HUMAN IDENTITY
The Image of God

TEXT: GENESIS 1:26–27

Then God said, "Let us make humankind in our image, according to our likeness; and let them have dominion over the fish of the sea, and over the birds of the air, and over the cattle, and over all the wild animals of the earth, and over every creeping thing that creeps upon the earth."

So God created humankind in his image,
in the image of God he created them;
male and female he created them.

Every temple needs an image. The creation, God's cosmic temple, is no different. At the climactic moment of creation, God placed an image in it. Humanity is the image of God. This is our fundamental identity as human beings.

But what does that mean?

At one level, it involves our embodied existence. We are the walking, talking, and breathing presence of God in the world. We do not live in the heavens or walk around in celestial bodies. We are earthy, made of the dust of the Earth. We belong to the Earth; we live material, physical lives. We are not made of gold and silver, or wood and stone, like the idols that populate other temples. We are flesh and blood, and it is as flesh and blood that we image God.

At another level, it involves our capacities for relationship, creativity, rationality, morality, and spirituality, among a host of other qualities. We are equipped to participate in God's own life. When we create, we participate in God's creative activity. When we live in intimacy with another, we participate in God's own community of love. When we act in love and seek justice, we participate in God's own nature. We are created to be like God, and God gave us the capacity to participate in God's own life.

God forbade Israel to make any idols or images of God. Those images would have no breath in them. God does not want human-made images because God has already made God's own image. God does not need another image because we are the image of God.

As divine image bearers, we represent God within the creation. Everything about us images God's own life. It is not one or two aspects that image God, but our whole selves represent God. Whether it is our creativity, our intellect, or our relationships, we are designed to represent God in every respect, and we are equipped to participate in God's mission.

This is our human identity. This is the status God gives us. We are God's representatives on the Earth. It is the essence of human dignity.

This means every human being participates in the life of God. We share the divine nature to the extent that we participate in God's own nature. We love because we are the image of God. We reason because we are the image of God. We know intimacy because we are the image of God. Our every breath is the breath of the Spirit of God, who gives us life, dignity, and status within God's good creation.

This means that every human person, no matter their ethnicity, nationality, gender, or age, has intrinsic dignity and worth. Every human person is crowned with glory and honor as the image of God. Everyone possesses royal nobility.

Every human being is valuable because they represent God. Consequently, we love and honor every human being because we love and honor God.

QUESTION: What does it mean to say, "I am created in the image of God," and how does this shape our lives as God's representatives on the Earth?

PRAYER: *Thank you, God, for sharing your life with us that we might become like you and represent you in the world.*

THE HUMAN VOCATION
Fill the Earth

TEXT: GENESIS 1:28

God blessed them, and God said to them, "Be fruitful and multiply, and fill the earth and subdue it; and have dominion over the fish of the sea and over the birds of the air and over every living thing that moves upon the earth."

As imagers of God, humanity represents God within the creation. That is our identity, and it includes a vocation, a calling. God invites humanity to participate in God's mission. Our identity equips us to partner with God as we execute that mission.

In the beginning, God blessed humanity as male and female and directed them to be fruitful, multiply, fill, and subdue the Earth, and exercise royal dominion over every living thing upon the Earth. That is our human vocation.

Our first calling is this: God blessed humanity so that we might fill the Earth.

This is a biological function, and it is most often heard as a divine invitation to have children. This means that sex is good, that procreation is good, and that God wants to populate the whole Earth with human beings. Consequently, we partner with God through procreation as we cocreate children with God's help.

Moreover, God wants to fill the whole Earth, and the diversity of the Earth entails the diversification of humanity. For example, people who live in Alaska cannot wear the same clothes, eat the same foods, or even develop the same rituals as people who live in Guatemala. The spread of humanity across the globe meant the rise of diverse cultures and people groups. This, too, is good.

At the same time, there is something more going on here than population growth and geographical expansion.

"Be fruitful and multiply, and fill the earth" is important language in the rest of the biblical story. When God called Abraham, God multiplied his descendants and filled the land of Canaan with them. While this involved biology, it is also significant that as Israel filled the land given them, they became a witness to the glory of God among the nations. God filled the land so that the glory of the Lord might permeate it through a people who imaged or represented God in that land.

God's goal is to fill the whole Earth with that glory. That glory is not found in mere population growth but in human flourishing. As the late second-century Christian martyr Irenaeus wrote (*Against Heresies*, Book IV.20.7), "The glory of God is a human being fully alive" (my translation). When we live out our identity as divine imagers and when human beings flourish throughout the Earth, the whole Earth is filled with God's glory. In this sense, "be fruitful and multiply," then, includes single people gifted by God for the sake of the kingdom of God (1 Cor. 7:7) and those who are eunuchs for the sake of the kingdom of God (Matt. 9:12).

Later in the biblical story, at Pentecost, God will pour out the Spirit upon Israel, and Israel will once again be fruitful and multiply (Acts 6:7; 12:24). As Israel grows and includes the nations in their community, the glory of the Lord will fill the Earth. Jesus, the Jewish Messiah, will one day fill all things with the glory of God.

As divine imagers, we are tasked to fill the Earth with God's glory. When humans image God and flourish, God is glorified. This is our vocation, our first calling.

QUESTION: In what ways, in addition to procreation, ought human beings to fill the Earth today?

PRAYER: *May the Earth, O Lord, be filled with your glory!*

THE HUMAN VOCATION
Subdue the Earth

TEXT: GENESIS 1:28

God blessed them, and God said to them, "Be fruitful and multiply, and fill the earth and subdue it; and have dominion over the fish of the sea and over the birds of the air and over every living thing that moves upon the earth."

As the image of God, we represent God in the world, and, therefore, we are invited to partner with God in what God is doing in the world. Our identity shapes our vocation.

We are called to multiply and fill the Earth with the glory of God. In addition, we are called to continue the divine work of creation by subduing the Earth.

To subdue the Earth is humanity's creative function. As Creator, God brought order out of chaos. Hovering over the waters enclosed in darkness, God brought order to an uninhabitable Earth, which was a chaotic void at the time. God subdued the Earth to provide habitable space, and then God filled that space with life.

Part of our human vocation is to continue this creative work, which Genesis calls subduing the Earth. Unfortunately, some believe "subdue" empowers humanity to exploit the Earth and deplete its resources. But to "subdue" is not a destructive task in which the Earth is scorched but a creative one in which the Earth is ordered and its habitable space is enriched so life might flourish.

The seven days of creation did not rid the cosmos of chaos. Even after the sixth day of creation, darkness still existed, the waters still existed, and a chaos figure—the serpent—entered Eden itself. God called the light good but not the darkness, God did not remove the waters but gave them boundaries, and outside Eden, the universe was not yet fully ordered. Not until the new heaven and new Earth appear will chaos disappear from the Earth, when there will be no more sea and no more night (Rev. 21:4; 22:3).

Until then, we partner with God to subdue the remaining chaos. This ordering includes things as diverse as domesticating a field for crops or goats for milk as well as developing software programs to bring order to a mass of data. We use technology to enrich our lives while, at the same time, we do not destroy the Earth with it.

This vocation extends to every aspect of human life. The arts (from music to literature to fine art) are expressions of human creativity that bring beauty and order out of what was previously unordered or chaotic.

To subdue the Earth means to partner in God's creative work; it does not mean abusing or exploiting the creation. Whatever chaos remains in the creation, humanity is called, in partnership with God, to subdue and order it so life might flourish.

This means no work is secular as if it were disconnected from our missional identity and vocation. Every good work participates in the mission of God if it is engaged in the process of ordering chaos or engages our vocation as divine imagers. Technology manages resources, medicine serves wholeness, and social structures shape community. This is our human vocation. We cocreate with God.

QUESTION: In what ways do you subdue the Earth without destroying it?

PRAYER: *Thank you, O God, for inviting us into the work of creation and gifting us with the capacity to create with you!*

THE HUMAN VOCATION

Rule the Earth

TEXT: GENESIS 1:28

God blessed them, and God said to them, "Be fruitful and multiply, and fill the earth and subdue it; and have dominion over the fish of the sea and over the birds of the air and over every living thing that moves upon the earth."

As the image of God, we represent God in the world, and thus we are invited to partner with God in what God is doing in the creation. Our identity shapes our vocation.

We are called to multiply and fill the Earth with the glory of God, and we are also called to continue the divine work of creation by ordering the remaining chaos within the creation. Further, we are invited to share God's dominion over the creation—to rule the Earth. This is humanity's royal vocation.

Too often we hear "dominion" in tyrannical, oppressive, militaristic, or manipulative ways, but this is not how God rules. As images of God, we rule in a way that mirrors God's own rule.

For example, Israel's royalty, though they did not always effectively do so, represented God to the nation. God wanted them to rule with justice and mercy. Psalm 72 reminds Israel what "dominion" means. It is the humble exercise of power in the service of mercy for the sake of others.

Their rule was supposed to be more like a shepherd than a dictator. Far from exploitation and abuse, God's imagers rule as servants who give life and empower life. They benevolently care for the creation rather than exploit it.

This gains greater clarity when we recognize that we are corulers with God. God shares God's own dominion with us. We are coworkers, junior partners, in God's enterprise.

Our mission is to develop the full potential of creation as we lovingly care for and gratefully enjoy it. We pursue familial, social, and communal peace as we embody the justice and mercy of God within creation.

People are called into multiple kinds of work or different careers. As corulers with God, we choose particular careers. We choose these careers as ways to love God, serve our neighbors, and shepherd the Earth. Through these careers, we participate in the mission of God.

Medical professionals partner with God in healing the sick. Teachers partner with God by imparting knowledge and wisdom. Software developers bring order out of chaos. Sanitation workers serve the Earth and the human community by fostering a clean Earth. Professionals in the legal community partner with God as they pursue justice. Environmental biologists partner with God as they preserve and care for the creation.

Partnering with God in the execution of the divine mission is ministry in the kingdom of God as God reigns over the creation. We share God's rule, and we exercise power within the creation. We use this power to serve rather than dominate. Nurses, teachers, counselors, biologists, sanitation workers, and lawyers corule with God. Through our careers, we are ministers and royal priests in the dominion of God, which is God's creation.

We are the image of God, and as imagers, we partner with God in filling the Earth with the glory of the Lord, ordering the remaining chaos within creation for the sake of life, and shepherding the Earth so life might flourish.

QUESTION: In what ways might we rule or shepherd the Earth that avoids exploitation but also develops the potential of creation?

PRAYER: *O Lord, with grateful hearts we ask, who are we that you have shared your dominion with us?*

TWO TREES
A Wisdom Story

TEXT: GENESIS 2:15–17

The Lord God took the man and put him in the garden of Eden to [serve and guard] it [as priests]. And the Lord God commanded the man, "You may freely eat of every tree of the garden; but of the tree of the knowledge of good and evil you shall not eat, for in the day that you eat of it you shall die."

Within God's cosmic temple, God created a place called Eden. This holy sanctuary had a garden. Don't imagine backyard tomatoes, but visualize something like the Gardens of Versailles, a royal garden with manicured trees, flowers, and water fountains. Agriculture and horticulture were not the point. God planted this garden for communion, joy, and rest. It was the holy of holies of the cosmic temple, and it was the place where God walked in fellowship with humanity within the creation.

Humanity, created out of the dust of the Earth, was placed in the garden to guard and serve it, much like the priests of Israel protected and ministered in the temple. This is another aspect of our human vocation: we are priests and priestesses. We lead the creation in the praise of God, and we serve God in God's holy space and guard that space.

In the heart of the garden were two trees: the tree of life and the tree of the knowledge of good and evil. One tree gave life, and the other, if eaten before its time, led to death. These trees are symbols in Hebrew Wisdom literature. The tree of life represents the wisdom to live long upon the Earth. The tree of the knowledge of good and evil represents a maturity to live wisely in the world by discerning the difference between two paths, between good and evil, between life and death. Children, or the inexperienced, do not yet have this wisdom, and, therefore, they must not eat from the tree.

Eden is like a wisdom play. Adam and Eve were inexperienced, like children who do not know how to live wisely in the world. They lacked maturity, knowledge, and discernment to make appropriate life-giving decisions, like what Proverbs calls the "simple" (Prov. 1:4). What they needed was wisdom. As children, learning to grow into wisdom, Adam and Eve were not yet prepared for knowledge. To download that knowledge without wisdom learned through life experience is like giving a six-year-old a nuclear weapon. It leads to disaster. God, therefore, forbade eating from the tree of the knowledge of good and evil. They were not yet mature enough for such knowledge.

The garden was a safe place, but it had risks. One was the tree of the knowledge of good and evil. Why was this tree in the garden at all? It represented both choice and the goal of maturity—that is, to be like God. Adam and Eve were free to choose. They could grow into the likeness of God by trusting, listening to, and walking with God, which ultimately led to the knowledge of good and evil. Or, they could act foolishly by eating too soon, and that led to death. The choice was theirs.

The story of Adam and Eve is our story. We all begin innocent, inexperienced, and immature. We grow by making choices, and we each, in some sense, have this freedom. These choices have real consequences. When we listen to wisdom and trust God's direction, there is life. When we listen to folly and distrust God's wisdom, there is death.

This is the human condition. Life and death lie before us, and we must choose a path. When we build on the sand of folly, our lives will collapse. When we build on the rock of wisdom, our lives will flourish. Alas, we typically don't know how to build well, and that is the next part of the story.

QUESTION: Where do you see wisdom and folly in the story of Adam and Eve?

PRAYER: *O God, give us the wisdom to participate in your life and advance your kingdom.*

HUMANITY TUMBLED

A Disordered Earth

TEXT: GENESIS 3:1–7

Now the serpent was more crafty than any other wild animal that the Lord God had made. He said to the woman, "Did God say, 'You shall not eat from any tree in the garden'?" The woman said to the serpent, "We may eat of the fruit of the trees in the garden; but God said, 'You shall not eat of the fruit of the tree that is in the middle of the garden, nor shall you touch it, or you shall die.'" But the serpent said to the woman, "You will not die; for God knows that when you eat of it your eyes will be opened, and you will be like God, knowing good and evil." So when the woman saw that the tree was good for food, and that it was a delight to the eyes, and that the tree was to be desired to make one wise, she took of its fruit and ate; and she also gave some to her husband, who was with her, and he ate. Then the eyes of both were opened, and they knew that they were naked; and they sewed fig leaves together and made loincloths for themselves.

When God began to create, God took what was unordered and ordered it to make a good, habitable space. God filled it with life, blessed it for growth and development, and gave humanity a choice.

This choice was highlighted by the presence of the serpent in the garden. The serpent was clever but was also a symbol of chaos in the ancient world. This crafty serpent was the presence of chaos in the garden.

But why did God permit chaos in the garden? Perhaps it highlighted freedom. The man and woman were free to choose, and chaos gave them space to choose. The snake probed them and offered what they wanted. They wanted to be like God—not because they were rebels but because their destiny was to be like God. They were created to become like God. God wanted them to discern between good and evil because this was part of what it meant to be like God.

The serpent, however, asked them to distrust God and take a short-cut to maturity. Like all children, they wanted to grow up fast. They grasped for wisdom as the serpent outwitted them. In their immaturity, they chose folly. Consequently, they failed to grow up. They circumvented the process that makes authentic wisdom and human flourishing possible. They did not maliciously rebel, but like any immature child, they failed to trust their parent, as all children have done since.

When they ate what was forbidden, they fell upward. They gained knowledge, but they were not ready for it. It burdened them with toxic shame, and they realized they were naked. Their distrust generated fear and mutual accusation. They gained knowledge but at a cost.

Consequences followed. Shortcuts sometimes have dire outcomes, and any shortcut to maturity is strewn with potholes and obstacles. Ill-equipped for knowledge, their choice introduced anxiety, brokenness, and fear.

While harmony once existed within Eden, hostility emerged between the serpent and the woman. While childbearing was originally free of anxiety, now the woman would bear children with great fear. While the original couple once knew harmony in their marriage, now they would experience conflict. While in the garden the man enjoyed a bountiful provision, now he would anxiously struggle with the ground to produce food. While in Eden, the man and woman were nourished by the tree of life, but now they would experience death.

These transitions were not so much punishments as direct consequences of foolish decisions. Folly led to self-destruction and death. The original couple did not trust God's timetable for maturity, and they rushed headlong into knowledge for which they were unprepared. As a result, they created a different world for themselves than the one God provided in Eden. This brought disorder and moral chaos into Eden.

These consequences were fully realized when they were exiled from the garden. Due to their folly, life was no longer innocent. But God responded with honesty and grace. God described the consequences and then graced them with clothing, preserved their lives east of Eden, and blessed them with children. The man and woman became Adam and Eve, as the man named Eve the mother of all living. This was no angry God, but a loving parent who practiced tough love with children who needed to learn how to live the hard way. Adam and Eve, like all humans since, needed to attend the school of hard knocks east of Eden.

QUESTION: When have you acted prematurely and foolishly rather than waiting for maturation and the clarity that comes from wisdom?

PRAYER: *Give us eyes to see you, O Lord, that we might practice your wisdom instead of our own.*

HUMANITY TUMBLED

Violence Enters the World

TEXT: GENESIS 4:3–7

In the course of time Cain brought to the Lord an offering of the fruit of the ground, and Abel for his part brought of the firstlings of his flock, their fat portions. And the Lord had regard for Abel and his offering, but for Cain and his offering he had no regard. So Cain was very angry, and his countenance fell. The Lord said to Cain, "Why are you angry, and why has your countenance fallen? If you do well, will you not be accepted? And if you do not do well, sin is lurking at the door; its desire is for you, but you must master it."

East of Eden, death lies ahead for everyone in Genesis except Enoch. It seems we have already hit rock bottom, with nowhere to go but the grave.

Death is not good, but it isn't the whole story. There is more to this picture. Things can get worse. Some things are worse than death.

Sin is worse than death. The word *sin* is not used to describe what happened in Eden, though it is generally applicable. The word first appears when God confronts Cain about his anger.

Cain was angry with God and envious of his brother because God did not accept his offering from the produce of his crops, though he did accept Abel's offering from the flock. We do not know exactly why

God did not accept it. Whatever the reason, Cain's anger put him at risk. "Sin," God said, "is lurking at the door; its desire is for you, but you must master it."

Sin, like a predator, stalks our hearts. It is an indwelling alien power. Sin wants to take hold of us, enslave us, and render us powerless. Sin wants to dominate, even devour, us. We all sense this; it is why we sometimes do things we don't want to do and perhaps never thought we would actually do.

When sin overpowers, we lose sight of God's purposes. We miss the mark. We fail to image or represent God in the creation. Sin turns our purpose and vocation toward something or someone other than God and God's mission.

Sin makes things worse. Cain moved from anger to violence because sin mastered him. When anger is conceived, it gives birth to violence. Jesus understood this. Whoever is angry with another, he said, has already committed murder (Matt. 5:22). Sin erupted in violence when Cain's angry heart lashed out at Abel, whose name means *futility* or *nothingness*. His brother's name came to life when Cain killed him. In the wake of Abel's murder, frustration and futility hovered over life east of Eden.

Violence breeds violence. Cain feared this. He thought others might take matters into their own hands and kill him. His fear recognized the inner dynamic of violence. Fueled by anger and generating fear, violence has no stopping point.

Yet, hope is always present within God's good creation, though it sometimes dims beyond recognition. We heard hope when Eve gave birth to Cain and gave him a name that expressed vitality and life. She blessed God with her confession: "I have produced a man with the help of the LORD" (Gen. 4:1).

Adam and Eve were not bound over to evil by their exclusion from Eden. By the grace of God, they bore children, raised crops, herded flocks, and worshiped the Lord. God did not remove grace from the creation. The Lord did not execute Cain but protected him; the Lord showed mercy. God's blessing continued, even in Cain, whose marriage produced children, and Cain built a city. Though living east of Eden, God's purposes for the world were still at work, and humanity not only multiplied but also created music, smelted metals, and built cities.

Cain's violence did not end the story any more than Adam and Eve's immature choice did. The story continues, and God continues to pursue humanity.

QUESTION: Where do you see grace and mercy in the story of Cain and Abel, and where do you see the degeneration of humanity?

PRAYER: *O God, give us the grace and power to love our neighbors.*

HUMANITY TUMBLED

Violence Encompasses the Earth

TEXT: GENESIS 6:11–13

Now the earth was corrupt in God's sight, and the earth was filled with violence. And God saw that the earth was corrupt; for all flesh had corrupted its ways upon the earth. And God said to Noah, "I have determined to make an end of all flesh, for the earth is filled with violence because of them; now I am going to destroy them along with the earth."

Violence breeds violence. Cain feared this. He thought others might take matters into their own hands and kill him. His fear recognized the inner dynamic of violence. Fueled by anger, violence has no stopping point, and it generates fear. Lamech, one of Cain's descendants, boasted about killing a young man who insulted him, and he imagined his fame was greater than his ancestor's. Lamech became a hero about whom songs were sung to celebrate his brutality (Gen. 4:23).

Violence, energized by sin, saturated the creation. As humanity multiplied, violence increased. When the "sons of God" and the "daughters" of men married, their children became *Nephilim* (Gen. 6:1–2). While the meaning of this term is variously interpreted, the *Nephilim* became mighty warriors or perhaps something like supermen in their culture. Their feats were renowned and violent. Not only did death reign, but sin also reigned as the Earth was filled with violence.

It got worse. It got so bad that God not only grieved the violence but had a change of mind. The violence pained God, and God felt it in God's own inner life, so much so that God changed in some way. God was horrified at what the world had become, which was the reason for the great flood God sent upon the world in order to cleanse and renew it. (Other ancient flood stories, like the Epic of Gilgamesh, gave a different reason—the gods annihilated humanity because they were annoyed by how loud they were!)

The intent of the story is to say something like this: When God saw how sin had exploded in the world and how it had a grip on every human heart, God uncreated the creation in order to start over. In other words, God changed in that God decided to bring order back to a world spinning out of control in chaotic violence. God decided to put things right and balance the books. In effect, God rebooted the creation because the world had crashed under the weight of its own violence.

At the same time, God chose Noah, whose name means *rest*, to lead the renewal of the new world, which would rise out of the floodwaters. Just as God blessed humanity in the beginning, when the waters receded, God blessed Noah's family with the same call: "Be fruitful and multiply, and fill the Earth" (Gen. 1:28). God's blessing infused new life into the original mission. Creation had a new beginning. The grace of God, including the gift of life itself, continued, and that grace renewed God's blessing and mission within creation.

There are traces of hope in this story. God stuck with us. However, in the wake of the excessive violence and evil in the past, God decided to shorten human life spans and institute a sacred boundary: whoever sheds blood, that one's blood will be shed (Gen. 9:6). The flood story is God's judgment on human violence.

God did not remove grace from the creation. The goodness of creation remained. The population, as God intended, multiplied. God wanted the mission to continue rather than implode. Though God's patience was long and deep, divine justice weighed in to adjust the balance. However, God did not annihilate the creation but renewed it. The mission of God continued.

QUESTION: Where do you see grace, hope, and righteousness in the story of the Noahic flood?

PRAYER: *O God, remove the violence embedded in our hearts that we might enjoy the goodness of your creation and the love of our fellow human beings.*

HUMANITY DEGENERATED

An Alternative Story

TEXT: GENESIS 11:2–4

And as they migrated from the east, they came upon a plain in the land of Shinar and settled there. And they said to one another, "Come, let us make bricks, and burn them thoroughly." And they had brick for stone, and bitumen for mortar. Then they said, "Come, let us build ourselves a city, and a tower with its top in the heavens, and let us make a name for ourselves; otherwise we shall be scattered abroad upon the face of the whole earth."

It seems God is a realist when it comes to humanity. The power of sin is deeply entrenched in human hearts. Even when God rebooted the creation through a flood, it did not cure the human heart of its ancestral sin. God knew violence would reappear because of the strong grip of sin. God, therefore, issued a warning: whoever sheds blood, their blood is at risk as well (Gen. 9:6). Jesus offered a similar caution: whoever lives by the sword will die by the sword (Matt. 26:52). Violence is a dead-end. No one wins.

But violence continued in many forms. Ham raped his father Noah. Civilizations rose and fell, and empires emerged. Babel is one of those ancient empire stories. The people decided to build a monumental city, with a tower reaching to the heavens, in order to establish their reputation.

The tower was no military lookout. It was a ziggurat. Many still exist in modern Iraq. They began to appear no earlier than the fourth millennium BCE and were continuously built into the first millennium BCE. The great city of Babylon, the namesake of Babel, featured a massive ziggurat dedicated to the god Marduk.

These structures were religious sanctuaries. They were temples for the gods, and they were where Earth touched the heavens. The problem with the Tower of Babel was neither its technology nor the unity of its people. Instead, the people of Babel erected a new sanctuary for the gods, gathered themselves around that sanctuary, and divested themselves of the divine mission to fill the Earth. They replaced Eden with a ziggurat. Babel stayed put, built an empire, and stoked its own ego. Babel committed idolatry, and thus God ended their cohesive civilization.

Humanity hit rock bottom. Babel reversed the divine mission in order to serve its own interests. Whereas God's words were "let us make humankind in our own image" (Gen. 1:27), Babel said, "let us make a name for ourselves" (Gen. 11:4). Whereas God's mission was to fill the Earth, Babel wanted to fill the heavens with its own presence. Humanity, represented by Babel, moved from violence to overt idolatry, from destroying fellow imagers with the sword to substituting themselves for God. They progressed in their depravity. Sin did its work, and humanity tumbled further east of Eden until it hit its nadir.

We all live east of Eden. Death reigns over us, and sin lurks in our hearts. Violence continuously erupts, empires still rule the Earth, and idolatry is pervasive. In some sense, we are still tumbling as violence and idolatry are perpetually invigorated by the power of sin in our lives and cultures. We stumbled out of Eden and tumbled from anger to violence, and then from violence to idolatry. We find ourselves mired in the muck of our own moral chaos despite God's persistent presence, coaxing, and mercy.

Due to God's mercy, however, hope is not lost. God's mission is still in play, and we create art, literature, and new technologies; build cities; marry; bear children; domesticate animals; grow crops; and spread across the globe. God's grace still empowers us with gifts and tools even though sin often distorts them.

The mercy of God persists, and the story is not yet finished. God's mission has not reached its goal. By God's grace, the creation will realize its full potential, humanity will flourish, and the glory of God will fill the Earth. That is the rest of the story, and it has only just begun.

QUESTION: What "Babels" have you built in your own life, and how is God's grace revealed to you in the middle of such edifices?

PRAYER: *Forgive us, O Lord, for our foolish ways.*

ACT TWO

ISRAEL

THE PROMISE TO ABRAHAM

TEXT: GENESIS 12:1–3, 7A

Now the Lord said to Abram, "Go from your country and your kindred and your father's house to the land that I will show you. I will make of you a great nation, and I will bless you, and make your name great, so that you will be a blessing. I will bless those who bless you, and the one who curses you I will curse; and in you all the families of the earth shall be blessed." . . . Then the Lord appeared to Abram, and said, "To your offspring I will give this land."

Whereas the empire of Babel determined to make its own name great, God decided to make Abraham's name great.

This contrast illustrates the two paths humanity might pursue. Babel chose ambition, pride, and self-actualization, but humanity's authentic path is found in God's promise and gracious work. Abraham heard God's call, believed God, and trusted God's leading.

When God called Abraham to leave his home country in Mesopotamia and led him into an unknown land, God initiated a new story to redeem humanity's tumble into imperial violence and idolatry. God called Abraham to inaugurate a new humanity in a new land. Rather than give up the goal of communion with human beings, God renewed the mission to effect that goal. God chose Abraham; God chose redemption over annihilation.

But how would God do this through Abraham? While there are different ways to parse out God's promise to Abraham, there are three essential components.

First, God would multiply the descendants of Abraham so they would be as innumerable as the sand on the seashore or the stars in the sky. Second, God would give the descendants of Abraham a land to inhabit where God would dwell with them. Third, God would bless all the peoples of the Earth through the descendants of Abraham.

When God called Abraham, this mission was not exclusively for Abraham or his children. It was also for the sake of the nations as well. Abraham was blessed so that he, through his descendants, might bless all peoples. God was never simply concerned about Abraham. Instead, God chose Abraham for the sake of the whole world. Embedded in the Abrahamic promise is a mission with both universal and cosmic purpose.

This promise was a new act of divine creation. What God promised Abraham was present at the beginning of the theodrama. God blessed humanity so it might be fruitful and multiply. God gave humanity land not only for its own habitation but also as a divine dwelling place. God intended to fill the Earth and include all humanity. The Abrahamic promise is the continuation of God's purpose in creation.

The Abrahamic promise intends to redeem what had previously degenerated into evil and violence. Ultimately, the promise will bless the nations through the Jewish Messiah, prepare a new heaven and new Earth as a home for the righteous (2 Pet. 3:13), and include all nations and peoples within the redeemed community. The Abrahamic promise finds its fulfillment in the work of Jesus the Jewish Messiah.

The Abrahamic promise is, well, a promise. It has no conditions; it is God's commitment to humanity through Abraham. God will accomplish what God had always intended to achieve—that is, the communion of God and humanity through life together upon the Earth.

God promised Abraham gifts, Abraham believed God, and God remained faithful to those promises. God's faithfulness is the rest of the story.

QUESTION: What does God's faithfulness to Abraham mean for our life with God today?

PRAYER: *We thank you, O God, for your faithfulness to Abraham.*

ISRAEL AS NEW HUMANITY

TEXT: EXODUS 6:2–8

God also spoke to Moses and said to him: "I am the Lord. I appeared to Abraham, Isaac, and Jacob as God Almighty, but by my name 'The Lord' I did not make myself known to them. I also established my covenant with them, to give them the land of Canaan, the land in which they resided as aliens. I have also heard the groaning of the Israelites whom the Egyptians are holding as slaves, and I have remembered my covenant. Say therefore to the Israelites, 'I am the Lord, and I will free you from the burdens of the Egyptians and deliver you from slavery to them. I will redeem you with an outstretched arm and with mighty acts of judgment. I will take you as my people, and I will be your God. You shall know that I am the Lord your God, who has freed you from the burdens of the Egyptians. I will bring you into the land that I swore to give to Abraham, Isaac, and Jacob; I will give it to you for a possession. I am the Lord.'"

God led the descendants of Abraham into Egypt, where they were eventually enslaved. Pharaoh oppressed them and killed Hebrew babies in order to suppress their numbers. Israel found themselves living in the moral chaos of the imperial power of Egypt. But God heard their cry and sent Moses to lead Israel out of slavery into freedom, to lead them out of the moral chaos into new life.

The Exodus, the liberation of Israel from Egypt, was the creation of Israel. From the moral and oppressive chaos of Egyptian slavery, God created a new people, a new nation. God gave humanity a new start. God gave birth to Israel, a people through whom God would display God's glory and call the nations into communion with God's own life.

God liberated Israel from slavery through God's creative power. The story of the crossing of the Red Sea is filled with creation language. From the chaos of the waters, God defeated the imperial powers arrayed against Israel, baptized a new people into Moses, and brought them safely through the waters into a new land. The Exodus birthed a new people.

Israel, as the firstborn among the nations, was created to serve as the renewed image of God in the world. In this sense, they were a new humanity. God rebooted the divine intent to fill the Earth with the glory of God by forming a people who would embody God's values and live in covenant relationship with God.

Israel was God's remnant among the nations. "You only have I chosen of all the families of the earth," God said in Amos 3:2 (NIV). While the prospects for humanity looked bleak in the early chapters of Genesis, God elected Israel as a nation among the peoples of the Earth to reveal God's identity.

Designed as the renewed image of God in the world, Israel was supposed to become what God had envisioned for humanity from the beginning. Just as humanity was originally placed in the Garden of Eden, so God placed Israel in a new Eden in the land God promised Abraham.

The new Eden, flowing with milk and honey, was created out of the moral chaos of Canaan and given to Israel as the place where they could flourish in peace and safety. The rains would water the crops, and they would enjoy the fruit of the harvest. The wild animals would not harm anyone in the land, and the security of the land rested in God's presence. The promised land was a new Eden for a new humanity. God graciously lived with Israel and walked among them as their God, just as God did in Eden. Israel no longer lived east of Eden; they lived in Eden.

God gave Israel the Torah to guide them in their new life with God. Yet, instead of leaning into God's wisdom, they often chose to follow the ways of the nations. They repeated the folly of Adam and Eve, with corresponding results. They, too, were exiled from Eden and ended up, once again, living east of Eden with the rest of us.

QUESTION: How does the theme of liberation look in your life, and what are some of the behaviors and thoughts from which you need liberation?

PRAYER: *God, we confess that only you can liberate us from our bondage, and we ask you to give us eyes to see our deep need and your wondrous grace.*

ISRAEL AS A ROYAL PRIEST AMONG THE NATIONS

TEXT: EXODUS 19:3–6

Then Moses went up to God; the Lord called to him from the mountain, saying, "Thus you shall say to the house of Jacob, and tell the Israelites: You have seen what I did to the Egyptians, and how I bore you on eagles' wings and brought you to myself. Now therefore, if you obey my voice and keep my covenant, you shall be my treasured possession out of all the peoples. Indeed, the whole earth is mine, but you shall be for me a priestly kingdom and a holy nation. These are the words that you shall speak to the Israelites."

Between their exodus from Egyptian slavery and their entrance into the new Eden, the land of promise, Israel encountered God at Mount Sinai. At God's holy mountain, God commissioned Israel as a royal priest among the nations.

At Sinai, God announced the good news of divine grace and entrusted Israel with a vocation. The good news is that God carried Israel on eagles' wings from Egypt to Sinai in order to begin a new relationship with them. God entered into covenant with them so they would become God's own possession. God would be their God, and they would be God's people. God blessed Israel with God's own presence and gave them status as God's firstborn among the nations.

This status came with responsibility. When God created humanity as the image of God, humanity was invested with the responsibility to fill the Earth with divine glory and care for it. In a similar way, when God created Israel, God entered into covenant with them, called them "my people" (Exod. 6:7), and invested them with responsibility, a mission, a vocation.

Like humanity in the beginning, this mission arose out of their role as royal priests. Just as humanity—as the image of God—is a royal priest within the creation, so Israel was a royal priest among the nations. As royalty, they represented God in the world. As God's ambassadors, they embodied the values and life of God in their own community. As priests, they mediated the presence and grace of God in the world. In their priestly role, Israel received God's blessing in order to bless the nations, and they invited the nations to hear the Word of the Lord.

God wanted Israel to showcase wisdom and understanding, to display divine glory and righteousness. The Torah was a witness to the nations, and if Israel lived by its guidance, the nations would say, as Deuteronomy 4:6 anticipated, "Surely this great nation is a wise and understanding people" (NIV). If Israel followed the Torah, they would embody wisdom, and they would show the nations how to live in peace, harmony, and justice. If Israel followed the Torah, Israel would flourish, and in their flourishing, they would commend God's wisdom to the nations.

The Great Commission of the Hebrew Bible, found in Isaiah 49:6, underscores Israel's missional purpose: they were a light for the nations and were appointed to bring God's salvation to the ends of the Earth. Israel was not simply a means by which God would send the Messiah but also a witness to the holy love of God among the nations.

As the image of God in the world, Israel served the nations as a city on a hill, a light in the darkness. At times, they succeeded, and at other times, they did not, just like us.

QUESTION: In what ways are you a light in the darkness?

PRAYER: *Forgive us, O Lord, when our light does not shine and the darkness overwhelms us.*

GOD DWELLS WITH ISRAEL

TEXT: EXODUS 40:34–38

Then the cloud covered the tent of meeting, and the glory of the Lord filled the tabernacle. Moses was not able to enter the tent of meeting because the cloud settled upon it, and the glory of the Lord filled the tabernacle. Whenever the cloud was taken up from the tabernacle, the Israelites would set out on each stage of their journey; but if the cloud was not taken up, then they did not set out until the day that it was taken up. For the cloud of the Lord was on the tabernacle by day, and fire was in the cloud by night, before the eyes of all the house of Israel at each stage of their journey.

Mount Sinai must have been an impressive, even startling, sight. Enveloped in darkness with flashes of lightning, Israel heard the thunder and even, on one occasion, the voice of God. They felt the rumblings of God's presence in tremors that rippled through the Earth's crust. This was God's holy mountain. God descended upon it, and the glory of the Lord appeared as a consuming fire.

We might imagine that this would have been the end of Israel's journey. They had arrived at the holy mountain, the place where God lives. But it would become the beginning of Israel's real journey, the journey through the wilderness to the promised land, as they carried the presence of God with them.

At Sinai, Israel waited. They waited forty days for Moses, and when Moses returned, their wait continued. Their wait, however, was no passive resignation. God gave Israel a task, and they prepared for the moment when God would come to dwell among them. They built a tabernacle, a portable sanctuary. Its portability was a hopeful sign because God would go with them on the journey through the wilderness. They built the tabernacle, they waited, and they prepared for what they could not even imagine.

This was Israel's Advent season. They were waiting for something, and perhaps they were not even sure what it was. They prepared a sanctuary, a worship center. They prepared themselves as they listened to Moses and obeyed his every instruction. They consecrated themselves to the service of God. They did everything they were commanded. They set up the tabernacle and finished the work.

Then it happened. The Lord drew near. The glory of God, the redemptive and personal presence of the Lord, filled the tabernacle. A cloud hovered over the tent while the consuming fire of God's presence filled the sanctuary. God now dwelt within Israel's camp. In a sense, God moved from the mountain to the tent. God moved from a permanent fixture to a portable one. The holy presence of the burning bush was now within a portable tent. God, too, was going on a journey, a journey with Israel.

Their wait was over. Advent had arrived. A new journey was beginning. God, the consuming fire present in the cloud, would lead and guide them. God would bring them to the promised land, and God's presence was their assurance and their strength.

Later, Israel would know this presence in a more permanent way through the temple, upon which God's glory would once again descend just as it had upon the tabernacle.

God filled the tabernacle, and then God filled the temple, just as God had, in the beginning, filled Eden and dwelt in the cosmic temple. This is the gift of divine presence; it is the gift of grace, mercy, and communion. Just as God rested on the seventh day of creation, so now God rested within Israel's tabernacle and then the temple. This was yet another move toward God's goal for the whole of creation, which is to include all peoples within the orbit of God's love and for God to dwell upon the Earth with them.

QUESTION: In what ways do you experience the presence of God?

PRAYER: *God, make yourself known to us so we might taste the sweetness of your love and goodness.*

ISRAEL INHERITS A LAND

TEXT: JOSHUA 11:23

So Joshua took the whole land, according to all that the Lord had spoken to Moses; and Joshua gave it for an inheritance to Israel according to their tribal allotments. And the land had rest from war.

God's intent is important. God gave a land to Israel so they might rest within it—to rest from war and with God. The goal was peace and communion through God's dwelling presence throughout the land.

The land was not a reward for Israel's military might or moral righteousness. It was an undeserved gifted based upon God's gracious promise to Abraham. It was an *inheritance*, a word that occurs, in some form, more than fifty-nine times in the Book of Joshua. Moreover, it was an inheritance not only for Israel's own benefit, but also for the sake of the nations.

Joshua's language points us to both creation and the future.

God's land gift to Israel is analogous to God's creation of the Earth. God gave the cosmos to Adam and Eve. God "put" (Gen. 2:15) them in the Garden of Eden to serve and protect it. Adam and Eve were priests in God's temple, God's home. This was God's inheritance for humanity. God created humanity so it might reign with God within the creation. Humanity was invited to live within the creation as God's partner in cocreating the future and co-shepherding the creation. Israel was given a land to partner with God in filling the Earth with God's glory.

This also anticipates the future. God will create the new heaven and new Earth as an inheritance for redeemed humanity. What Israel inherited in the Book of Joshua is precisely the type of inheritance God will give to humanity. A day was coming when not only Israel would represent the heritage of God, but also Egypt and Assyria would be God's people and the work of God's hands (Isa.19:25). A day was coming when the meek would inherit the Earth (Matt. 5:5).

God gave the land, and God gave rest. At the same time, Israel was an active agent—God's coworker—in the process by which the land came to rest from its wars. Israel defeated many kings (Josh. 12), but much of the land was not yet in their possession (Josh. 3). They did not annihilate the people in the land, but they, by God's grace, cleared space for the holy dwelling of God upon the Earth through subduing the chaos present in the land (Josh. 18:1).

Just as God placed humanity in Eden and they were told to subdue the chaos on the rest of the Earth (Gen. 1:28), so God's people even now (like Israel before them) are given the task of subduing the chaos. Within the story of Jesus, this task is not a violent one but rather the pursuit of peace and righteousness. Disciples of Israel's Messiah subdue the chaos (sin and unrighteousness) through redemptive suffering instead of violent revolution. Rest for all peoples will emerge through love and kindness as God renews all things through Jesus.

Our present kingdom task is to subdue the chaos through practicing peace as peacemakers. And God promises to renew the Earth and create a new heaven and new Earth where righteousness and peace dwell (2 Pet. 3:13).

In this way, God will fulfill the promise to Abraham. The land Abraham was promised was a promissory note to humanity regarding the inheritance of the nations. Abraham was the "heir of the cosmos" (Rom. 4:13). In Abraham's seed, in the Messiah, we have become the heirs of Abraham (Gal. 3:29). We are the heirs of the cosmos, and in the new heaven and new Earth we shall inherit the Earth and enter into the fullness of God's rest.

QUESTION: In what way is land still part of our inheritance as disciples of Jesus, and what does this mean for our discipleship and hope?

PRAYER: *Thank you, dear Lord, for the gift of this Earth and the promise of a new heaven and a new Earth!*

ISRAEL WANTS A NEW KING

TEXT: 1 SAMUEL 8:4–9

Then all the elders of Israel gathered together and came to Samuel at Ramah, and said to him, "You are old and your sons do not follow in your ways; appoint for us, then a king to govern us, like other nations." But the thing displeased Samuel when they said, "Give us a king to govern us." Samuel prayed to the Lord, and the Lord said to Samuel, "Listen to the voice of the people in all that they say to you; for they have not rejected you, but they have rejected me from being king over them. Just as they have done to me, from the day I brought them up out of Egypt to this day, forsaking me and serving other gods, so also they are doing to you. Now then, listen to their voice; only—you shall solemnly warn them, and show them the ways of the king who shall reign over them."

Israel was designed as a theocracy without a human monarchy. There was no king over the nation except God.

God liberated Israel from Egypt, dwelt among them, gave them a land, and intended to lead Israel through Torah, prophets, and communal leaders (judges and elders, for example). Through their dependence upon God, Israel was called to live a distinct way of life by which it would bless the nations.

It was an anti-monarchical constitution of shared leadership, with an alternative approach to national security different from the nations. There was no standing army, but only untrained occasional militias to serve the homeland. This intentional incompetency highlighted the people's dependence upon God.

However, for the most part, Israel did not embrace its calling as God's people. Instead, they suffered the consequences of forsaking God. They were often oppressed. Sometimes they repented and God liberated them. But the cycle repeated itself over and over again until it spiraled into utter depravity, including horrific violence against women that highlighted their degeneracy.

Instead of depending upon God and following the Torah, "all the people did what was right in their own eyes" (Judg. 17:6, 21:25). Moral chaos reigned.

Israel diagnosed its problem. They did not have a king who could protect them from their enemies, reform the corruptions in communal leadership, and maintain law and order. What they needed was a human ruling authority, a monarchial politic.

In effect, they rejected God's theocratic rule in favor of the politics of the nations. They exchanged God's politic for another. They wanted a king.

The people chose the nations over God even though it was their own faithlessness and violence that subverted God's desire to give them rest in the land. They thought a king would protect them. Seemingly, they wrested control from God and placed it in the hands of a king. They gave their allegiance to a king rather than God.

But kings do not have the best interest of the people at heart. They conscript workers and soldiers. They build palaces in their own honor and seize daughters for their own use. They train the nation for war and keep them at war in order to maintain their own power and security.

The Torah warned about the rise of kings, the prophets railed against their abuse of power, the historians negatively assessed their reigns, and the poets longed for authentic justice.

The monarchy was not a solution but a detour. It was a grand experiment destined to fail because God knows human hearts. Violence and injustice are the tools of government for the sake of government. Israel's monarchy collapsed under its own weight of corruption and violence.

In response, God exiled Israel, ended the monarchy, and scattered the people among the nations. Israel became a diaspora. Instead of enlightening the nations through their national existence in the land, they would now become a light living among the nations.

Isaiah's servant songs offer a new vision for Israel's calling. They transform kingship into servanthood. This is God's answer to the demise of the monarchy, a failed project.

Israel would have a king—not one, however, who ruled through coercion and violence, but through loving service. A suffering servant would ultimately sit on the throne of David and transform it as the Prince of Peace who subdues the nations through giving himself as a ransom instead of employing violence against the nations. Israel's Messiah would be that kind of king.

QUESTION: Why was having a human king a bad idea for Israel?

PRAYER: *We confess, O God, that you reign over the Earth, and we pledge our allegiance to your kingdom.*

GOD'S GIFT TO ISRAEL

TEXT: ROMANS 9:4–5

They are Israelites, and to them belong the adoption, the glory, the covenants, the giving of the law, the worship, and the promises; to them belong the patriarchs, and from them, according to the flesh, comes the Messiah, who is over all, God blessed forever. Amen.

The most gut-wrenching expression of Paul's love for his own nation is found in Romans 9:1–5. Much of Israel, though gifted by God with wondrous privileges, had rejected God's Messiah. Paul was heartbroken as he listed the gifts in an overflow of praise for God's grace toward Israel. He named six gifts.

The first gift was adoption. God adopted Israel and gave them an inheritance—a double inheritance because Israel was God's child, the firstborn among the nations.

The second gift was the divine glory—the Shekinah glory that settled on the tabernacle and the temple. God gave that redemptive presence to Israel in a unique way, unlike how God related to other nations. God came to rest within Israel and walked among them.

The third gift was the covenants. God entered into a succession of covenants with Israel. Beginning with the Abrahamic promise, God then initiated a covenantal relationship with Israel through the Mosaic covenant. God mediated his grace and mercy through the priestly Levitical covenant and assured Israel of their perpetuity through the Davidic covenant. The covenants meant God was committed to Israel and enjoyed communion with them.

The fourth gift was the Torah. God gave the Torah to Israel as a gracious gift. It was not primarily a legal code but guidance for how to become the image of God in the world as a nation. The Torah guided Israel as they walked with God in the land of promise.

The fifth gift was temple worship. The temple (or literally, the liturgical service), with all the festivals and rituals connected to it, was God's generous invitation to enjoy communion through songs, prayer, sacrifices, and the eating of sacrifices at communal meals. The temple was God's gracious but holy presence among the people. It was the place where Israel came before the face of God as an assembly of praise.

The sixth gift was the promises. God promised Abraham a great nation, a land, and that his seed would bless the nations. God promised David that his descendants would sit on Israel's throne forever. God promised restoration to an exiled Israel. God promised a new heaven and a new Earth, which is yet to come.

The Messiah, who came from Abrahamic ancestry, was the one through whom the nations would also receive these gifts. These gifts now belong to the nations, to everyone who trusts in the Messiah. Through Abraham's messianic seed, we may all become children of Abraham by faith in Jesus because of the Messiah's faithfulness.

We, too, are adopted into the family of God. We, too, experience the divine glory as the Holy Spirit dwells in us. We, too, participate in the covenants as both Abraham's children and subjects of the son of David. We, too, receive the Torah as Scripture to guide our lives. We, too, assemble before God to praise and serve the God of Israel as a gathered people. We, too, are heirs of the promises of God to Israel.

We, through the faithfulness of the Messiah, have been grafted into Israel's tree; and these gifts, praise God, now belong to all who confess Jesus is Lord.

QUESTION: Which gift to Israel do you find particularly helpful in your understanding of your own experience with God?

PRAYER: *God, you gifted Israel out of your great love, and we confess with gratitude that this gifting is also a love for us.*

GOD'S TORAH
A Path to Life

TEXT: PSALM 19:7–10

The law of the Lord is perfect,
reviving the soul;
the decrees of the Lord are sure,
making wise the simple;
the precepts of the Lord are right,
rejoicing the heart;
the commandment of the Lord is clear,
enlightening the eyes;
the fear of the Lord is pure,
enduring forever;
the ordinances of the Lord are true
and righteous altogether.
More to be desired are they than gold,
even much fine gold;
sweeter also than honey,
and drippings of the honeycomb.

Psalm 19 identifies two forms of divine speech. One is nonverbal, natural, and experienced through the wonder present in God's creation (Ps. 19:1–6). The other is verbal.

God had spoken in history and entered into covenant with Israel. That story is told in the Torah. Those words are read in the assembly of

God's people. Israel had been given the "oracles of God" (Rom. 3:2), and this came, most foundationally, in the form of Torah.

Torah ("law") heads the praise of this divine speech in Psalm 19. It is the controlling metaphor for the other descriptions: decrees, precepts, and commandments. Those terms are couched in the framework of Torah, and Torah was not primarily a legal code but a story that guided Israel as it walked with God. Torah was instruction and guidance through narrative rather than primarily specific case law or isolated commands.

Embedded within the Torah are guidelines, directions, and formative practices that transform people into the image of God. As the psalmist declares, the Torah

- restores the soul as it renews life.
- makes the simple wise as it guides the inexperienced and immature.
- gives joy to the heart as it frees us from the anxiety and burdens of life.
- enlightens the eyes as it illuminates what human flourishing really is.

The Torah provides a path for healthy, joyful, and wise living.

The phrase "making wise the simple" (Ps. 19:7) is particularly significant. This is the language of Proverbs 1:1–7. Life has two paths: the foolish and the wise. But the "simple" are often too inexperienced to discern the difference. The Hebrew term for *simple* does not refer to a mental deficiency but to a lack of life experience. The "simple" are easily deceived, are driven by their desires, and act on impulse rather than judicious reflection. They react instead of respond to situations. Due to a lack of experience, their discernment is impaired or underdeveloped.

The Torah serves as a wise sage to help the "simple" discern good from evil, make choices, and understand the consequences of the different paths life can take. In other words, the Torah—God's guidance—is for their own good and for the good of the community in which they live. It is not an oppressive legal chain around the neck, but divine wisdom spoken for the sake of human health and well-being.

As a result, the wise response is submission, or, in the language of wisdom, it is to fear (awe, trust, or revere) the Lord. The fear of the Lord is the beginning of wisdom, and this humble submission and reverent respect for God calls us to embody the wisdom of the Torah in our own lives.

It is little wonder, then, that the psalmist regards God's speech as more valuable than gold or silver and sweeter than honey. This speech is about life, authentic life. A discerning, wise life has better consequences than hoarding gold or silver. It is much sweeter than the momentary taste of honey.

QUESTION: How is the Torah a positive part of our life with God?

PRAYER: *Thank you, O God, for your guidance!*

THE ORACLES OF GOD

TEXT: ROMANS 3:1–2

Then what advantage has the Jew? Or what is the value of circumcision? Much, in every way. For in the first place the Jews were entrusted with the oracles of God.

Though Paul did not mention this gift in Romans 9:1–5, earlier in the letter he had noted that Israel was entrusted with the very words of God. Israel was the keeper of the record of God's mighty acts.

Scripture does not drop out of the sky. On the contrary, the collection of holy writings called Scripture grew and developed over time within the course of Israel's history. Scripture was produced as part of the process of redemptive history and was intimately connected to Israel's status as a covenant nation.

God used covenantal messengers to guide Israel. The Torah provided the foundational covenant history and covenantal instruction. The prophets called people to faithful obedience to the covenant, warned Israel of its failures, and encouraged Israel with hopeful promises. Prophets, among others, recorded covenantal histories that bore witness to the history of God's relationship with Israel. The singers and sages of Israel provided liturgy and wisdom for life in Israel.

The holy writings emerged throughout the history of Israel as a way of grounding Israel in its past, guiding it in its present, and providing hope for its future. They were bound up with Israel's history and status as the covenant people of God. The Scriptures were God's unique gift to Israel and through Israel to the nations.

These are the "Holy Scriptures" which Paul commended to Timothy as "able to make" him "wise for salvation through faith in Christ Jesus" (2 Tim. 3:15 NIV). These are the texts Paul described as breathed out by God (or, inspired by God) and "profitable for teaching, for rebuking, for correcting, and for training in righteousness, that" every person called by God may be competent, "equipped for every good work" (2 Tim. 3:17 NIV).

Scripture, in general, serves a covenantal function, which is expressed through diverse genres and occasions. Scripture essentially administered the divine covenant with God's people and was thus normative for how they lived in covenant with God in the different cultures and situations in which people then lived.

Scripture bears witness to, interprets, and applies the saving work of God to the people of God. It narrates the redemptive work of God, interprets that work for us, and applies its meaning and significance to its original hearers. Though Scripture was written *to* those who received it in the past, it was also written *for* future believers.

As covenant people, we are guided by the covenant witness of Scripture. It bears witness to God's acts of redemptive love and calls us into relationship with God. It instructs and guides the people of God; it casts a vision for how to live out our identity as the representatives of God in the world.

This witness, as we have it now in the whole of the prophetic and apostolic testimony, is rooted in the saving acts of God that inaugurate a new creation. Jesus himself is the witness to God's saving work and the embodiment of the covenantal principles that shape all service to God. Jesus, as incarnate God, is the image of God, the true Israel, and the true human. He is the fundamental pattern for our life before God. And Scripture, ultimately, bears witness to him, the redeemer of Israel and the mediator between God and humanity.

QUESTION: What is the function of Scripture?

PRAYER: *We love your oracles, O God; thank you!*

THE WITNESS OF HISTORY

TEXT: 1 CHRONICLES 29:29–30

Now the acts of King David, from first to last, are written in the records of the seer Samuel, and in the records of the prophet Nathan, and in the records of the seer Gad, with accounts of all his rule and his might and of the events that befell him and Israel and all the kingdoms of the earth.

Every nation has a history. Each tells its story. National stories shape how they understand themselves and see their role in the world and in history. Israel was no different.

The prophets were Israel's storytellers. Typically, we think of prophets as preachers, but they were also historians. More specifically, they were covenantal messengers.

When God rescued Israel from Egyptian slavery, God entered into relationship with them through a covenant or pact. God raised up prophets to hold Israel accountable to that covenant.

At times, the prophets functioned like covenantal prosecutors who sued Israel on behalf of God as a way of calling them back into faithful relationship, and at other times, the prophets served a parental role, guiding Israel and offering hope. At still other times, the prophets were historians who kept records and explained the history between God and Israel. They wrote covenantal histories.

For example, the books of the Bible called Samuel, Kings, and Chronicles are based on the annals of various kings written by prophets. They tell the story of God's covenant relationship with God's people. To illustrate, Kings and Chronicles cover the same period from the reign of Solomon to the Babylonian exile but were written in different settings, with different purposes, and for different audiences.

Kings was written during the Babylonian exile. Their questions were, *Why are we here? Did the Babylonian gods overrule the God of Israel? Where are God's promises to Abraham and David?* Kings focuses on the sins of Israel and Judah. David and Solomon did not escape discipline, and the whole nation was judged for its sins. Judah was in exile because she, as God's wife, did not keep covenant with God. The Babylonian gods did not win. Rather, God removed Judah from her homeland, just as God exiled Adam and Eve from Eden for their folly. The prophet historians of Kings explain God's judgment.

Chronicles, on the other hand, was written after the exile at a time when some had returned from Babylon to their homeland. The postexilic questions were different. They asked, *Will God still dwell among us in this new temple? Will God take us back into covenant relationship? Will God still keep the promises made to Abraham and David?* Chronicles stresses God's yearning to restore a relationship with Israel. God will keep the promises made to Abraham and David, and God will dwell once again in the midst of Israel, just like at Sinai, the tabernacle, and the Solomonic temple. God is gracious to those who seek God's face. If the postexilic community seeks God, God will dwell among them once again. God seeks seekers.

God disciplined but also yearned for Israel. Israel's history speaks of God's severity but also of God's mercy. God pursued Israel and continually called them into renewed relationship. God will never forget them any more than a mother can forget her children. This is the story of God and Israel. It is the story of God and humanity. We forget, but God does not.

QUESTION: What is your own family story, and how does it shape you even now?

PRAYER: *Lord, may we learn from the stories of your people!*

THE HYMNS AND PRAYERS OF ISRAEL

TEXT: PSALM 19:14

Let the words of my mouth and the meditation of my heart
be acceptable to you,
O Lord, my rock and my redeemer.

We humans live in space and time, and we create space and time for what is important to us. The God of Abraham did this for Israel through the introduction of times for corporate worship in holy spaces.

Through weekly, monthly, and annual festivals, God provided Israel with a rhythm of worship and prayer that included times of celebration and joy as well as times of lament and repentance. Out of the chaos of their lives, God ordered time and space through various rituals in order to remind Israel who God was, to commune with God, to celebrate their life with God, to hear the story of God again, and to bring the stuff of real life into God's presence.

The Psalter, Israel's hymnbook and prayer book, expressed the fullness of their life with God, from its joys to its hurts. For centuries, Israel prayed and sang these words in the presence of God, and Jesus the Messiah, along with the church that followed him, also prayed and sang these life-giving and sometimes desperate words.

The psalms mirror the soul and give expression to intense feelings of lament and praise. They express confidence in God and our desire to worship the Creator, as well as our commitment to follow God's Torah. They express our deepest moments of despair and doubt. They confess sin, and they also question God's faithfulness in the midst of injustice and pain.

The psalms are a collection of diverse hymns, songs, and prayers that reflect the continuum of life. They move from confidence to lament to praise. They retell the history of God's people, pray for God's deliverance, and offer thanks for God's redemptive acts. These prayers have sustained the people of God through despair and triumph, through good times and bad.

Lament and praise are constants throughout the psalms. Almost half of the psalms are laments. They lament injustice, death, sickness, sin, and oppression. They ask God gut-wrenching questions like, "Why do you hide yourself in times of trouble?" (Ps. 10:1), "How long will you hide your face from me?" (Ps. 13:1), and "O Lord, do you cast me off?" (Ps. 88:14).

The suffering is real, and so are the questions. The laments are honest prayers about real life, and they reflect the deep sorrow that life often brings. We are invited to pray these laments with Israel. Jesus prayed them, even on the cross. God invites us to speak our hearts, and God promises to hear, just as God heard Jesus and answered his prayer through deliverance.

Praise is the other half of Israel's hymnbook. Sometimes this praise expresses quiet confidence like "The Lord is my shepherd" (Ps. 23:1) or "God is our refuge and strength" (Ps. 46:1). At other times, this praise evokes shouts of joy and thanksgiving. "I love the Lord," the psalmist shouted, "because [God] has heard my voice" (Ps. 116:1). Or, "Enter [God's] gates with thanksgiving" (Ps. 100:4).

The constant throughout all the psalms, even the psalms of lament, is the steadfast love of God and the hope that God will save. This is the confession of Israel. We bring our lives before God in worship, and God is faithful. God will hear, and God will deliver. That is the world the psalms ultimately project, which we enter to worship the God of Israel.

QUESTION: How have songs and prayers, including the psalms, shaped your own experience of life?

PRAYER: *O God, we protest the evil that is the world, and we praise you for your goodness; may your goodness reign!*

WISDOM AND FOLLY

TEXT: PROVERBS 9:9–10

Give instruction to the wise, and they will become wiser still;
teach the righteous and they will gain in learning.
The fear of the Lord is the beginning of wisdom,
and the knowledge of the Holy One is insight.

Wisdom and folly are personified as women in Proverbs 9. The wise sage of Proverbs portrays Lady Wisdom and Dame Folly as hostesses who invite those who pass by into their homes. The wise teacher encourages the simple, those who are inexperienced and do not have enough life experience under their belt, to make informed choices, to heed the voice of Lady Wisdom and reject Dame Folly's invitation.

Wisdom built her own house; she built creation itself as God created the world through her (Prov. 8). Wisdom is prepared. She sacrifices her own meat, mixes her own wine, and sets her own table. But Folly is loud—a good show but no substance. She is simple and ignorant—she does not know how to help. She has no resources of her own but roars with her own boisterousness.

Wisdom is active. She actively seeks people. She sends people out to gather them. Folly waits for others to find her (and she is not hard to find). They are both visible, but they have different methods. Folly waits for the simple to fall into her trap.

Wisdom offers her own bread and wine. She gives out of her own resources. Folly, however, offers stolen water and eats bread in secret.

Wisdom's invitation is public, open, and transparent. Folly invites us to secrecy and isolation. We are reminded how addictions (drugs, alcohol, and sex, for example) find vitality in secrecy and isolation. They bring death.

Wisdom urges us to live in her light, to walk through life with her insight. But folly makes no promises. In foolishness, we are awakened to the reality that the guests at her banquet inhabit *Sheol*. Wisdom brings life, but folly brings death.

We live in a creation built by God's wisdom. It is best to live by that wisdom, and the beginning of that wisdom is the fear of the Lord. When we live within the creation in ways that embody wisdom, we experience life with more serenity. But when we live within the creation in foolish ways, then we experience chaos and turmoil. God made the world so that round pegs fit round holes, but when, in our foolishness, we try to put a round peg into a square hole, something breaks. We break. The creation is built for a particular kind of living—that is, living by the fear of the Lord. Any other kind of living leads to brokenness.

Jesus said something similar at the end of the Sermon on the Mount (Matt. 7:13–14). The gate is wide and the road is broad that leads to destruction, but the gate is small and the road narrow that leads to life. It is the difference between life and death, the difference between wisdom and foolishness.

According to Jesus, a wise person builds a house on the rock—like the wisdom in the Sermon on the Mount. But foolish people build their houses on sand. The former house, built by wisdom, stands strong, but the house built on foolishness collapses. Alas! We have often found it much easier to sing the children's song than to heed its advice.

QUESTION: How have you wavered between wise and foolish choices?

PRAYER: *O God, give us the wisdom to discern between the path that leads to life and the path that leads to death.*

LIVING IN CHAOS

TEXT: ECCLESIASTES 1:2–3

Vanity of vanities, says the Teacher,
vanity of vanities! All is vanity.
What do people gain from all the toil
at which they toil under the sun?

Living within God's creation is both frustrating and delightful. Qoheleth, the wise teacher in Ecclesiastes, offers an extended reflection on this conundrum.

Life is absurd. The Hebrew word *hebel* (vanity) describes this frustration, and Qoheleth uses it thirty-seven times. Literally, it means *vapor*—like a breath in the cold air. Metaphorically, it means *futility*. As such, it communicates the seeming pointlessness of life.

The word, however, has more punch than this. It encompasses the unfathomable nature of life, the deep impenetrable mystery of life and death. Some suggest *enigma*, and life is enigmatic because we simply do not know. We are limited in perspective, and we cannot make sense of life.

Some suggest *absurd*. Life is frustrating. The seemingly ceaseless, circular, and pointless merry-go-round of life has no goal, no meaning, and no worth. Life, because of death, is hauntingly absurd.

What lies behind Ecclesiastes is the story in Genesis 3–11. When Qoheleth probes life, the teacher evokes the narrative world of Abel. The name Abel is the same word as *hebel*. The seemingly pointless, absurd, and unjust death of Abel at the hands of Cain symbolizes human existence in a world enslaved to death. Our lives are like Abel's life.

This is why it is good for us to sit with Ecclesiastes for a season rather than move on too quickly. Sometimes we are forced to do so when chaos assaults human life. We recoil at the death of children in tornadoes. We are shocked when children are killed in mass shootings. We despair over a virus that kills millions. Sometimes all we can do is agree with Qoheleth: *everything is absurd!*

Yet, without forgetting that life is *hebel*, Qoheleth also confesses that God has invested creation with joy and value. Though disoriented by the absurdity of life, Qoheleth remembers the Creator (Eccles. 12:1) and knows that "whatever God does endures forever" (Eccles. 3:14). Qoheleth holds these two truths in tension: Life is absurd, and God is the Creator. At the same time, Qoheleth confesses, no one knows "the work of God, who makes everything" (Eccles. 11:5). Life is an enigma.

Though life is filled with futility, we also experience God's good creation. Somehow and in some way, God gives joy in the midst of absurdity. Even in the midst of the hurt and pain of life, Qoheleth commends joy. "Go, eat your bread with enjoyment," the wise sage advises, "drink your wine with a merry heart" (Eccles. 9:7) and "enjoy life with your" spouse (Eccles. 9:9 NIV).

Qoheleth, while observing the absurdity of life, affirms Israel's confession of the theodrama. As Creator, God shares many good gifts with humanity, and God invites humanity to enjoy them. Though labor has become burdensome "toil," humanity may yet find joy in the work or vocation God gave them in the beginning. Though wealth is often used to oppress others, humanity may yet enjoy it as the gift of God. Though many may abuse both wine and spouses, they are God's good gifts within creation.

Life is both *hebel* and filled with the gifts of the Creator. We lament and recognize the absurdity of human existence, but we also receive God's good gifts in creation with gratitude and joy. Qoheleth does not reject God's creation. Instead, the wise teacher cries out for the full realization of God's reign within it.

There is much to grieve in our world: mass shootings, suicides, racism, sexism, homophobia, viruses, deaths, rapes, and abuse of power. We lament, and we call it *hebel*. *Hebel* happens!

And, without diminishing or minimizing the pain of our laments, we affirm the goodness of creation: the joy of food, wine, companionship, vocation, children, and life.

There is *hebel*, and there is good. Something is terribly wrong with this world, and something is wonderfully good about it, too.

For now, we lament the *hebel*, and we enjoy the good.

QUESTION: How have you experienced *hebel* but also the goodness of God?

PRAYER: *We acknowledge, O God, that life is hebel, but we trust in your goodness as the Creator.*

THE PROPHET AMOS CALLS FOR JUSTICE AND HOPE

TEXT: AMOS 5:15, 24

Hate evil and love good,
and establish justice in the gate;
it may be that the LORD, the God of hosts,
will be gracious to the remnant of Joseph. . . .
But let justice roll down like waters,
and righteousness like an ever-flowing stream.

How might a migrant worker convict luxurious homeowners about their oppressive lifestyles? What might a poor, rural believer say to wealthy, urban idolaters? This is the context in which Amos lived.

Amos was neither trained as a prophet nor assumed the career of a prophet. He was a shepherd in the Judean wilderness near Bethlehem and was from the backwater village of Tekoa. He supplemented his income by cultivating sycamore fig trees. He was a migrant worker, since those trees did not grow in the area of Tekoa.

The eighth century BCE was a time of prosperity and peace. Jeroboam II ruled over the northern kingdom, while Uzziah reigned over Judah. Jeroboam II had the longest reign of any northern king, and Uzziah had the second longest of any southern king. Together, their reigns approximated the "golden age" of Solomon himself in terms of territory, building projects, and economic trade.

Peace and prosperity, however, did not form a just and faithful nation. On the contrary, wealth was increasingly concentrated the hands of an elite few. Whereas their blessings should have blessed all, the wealthy used their blessings on themselves instead of sharing them.

The shepherd Amos went from his rural environs near Tekoa to the heartland of Israel's ruling elite in Bethel and Samaria. His message decried injustice, oppression, and idolatry. He announced Israel's future—one of both judgment and hope.

How do the poor speak a word from God to the rich? How does a lowly shepherd address the ruling class about their nation?

We want to stand with Amos as he speaks against injustice and idolatry. But we will miss the message if we do not become Amos's audience as well. We must hear Amos as those who live in luxury with more wealth than we need. Otherwise, we will simply make excuses and judge his words inapplicable—much like Israel responded to Amos.

Prosperity often creates spiritual apathy, along with greed and covetousness (as we always want more). If nothing else, the words of Amos warn us that prosperity is only a blessing if it is received with gratitude and shared. Otherwise, it becomes the root of greed, injustice, and oppression.

Nevertheless, Amos offered hope to Israel. In chapter 9, Amos announced good news: a day would come when God would renew Israel and fully restore relationship with them. God would again raise the tent of David, and a son of David would once again reign over the land.

Amos 9:11–15 offers hope not only to Israel but to the nations. The restoration of the "booth of David" includes the nations (Acts 15:12–21). They, too, will be called by the name of God. When that day arrives, the glory of the Lord will fill the whole Earth and the meek will inherit the Earth. The Abrahamic promise will be fulfilled when the whole Earth becomes the Lord's. Both Israel and the nations will enjoy the land, the blessings of the covenant, and the presence of God when the "booth of David" is restored. That story is the next act in the theodrama.

QUESTION: What are some of the spiritual idolatries of our time and some of the spiritual adulteries of the church?

PRAYER: *Give us the courage, O Lord, to follow the example of your servant Amos and proclaim your righteousness to your people and to the nations!*

THE PROPHETS CALL FOR JUSTICE

TEXT: ZECHARIAH 7:9–12

Thus says the Lord *of hosts: Render true judgments, show kindness and mercy to one another; do not oppress the widow, the orphan, the alien, or the poor; and do not devise evil in your hearts against one another. But they refused to listen, and turned a stubborn shoulder, and stopped their ears in order not to hear. They made their hearts adamant in order not to hear the law and the words that the* Lord *of hosts had sent by his spirit through the former prophets. Therefore great wrath came from the* Lord *of hosts.*

The earlier prophets, Zechariah announced to postexilic Judah, delivered the Word of the Lord to their ancestors. The Lord, through the Spirit of God, sent word after word to various prophets in the preexilic era, but Israel did not listen.

Zechariah describes Israel with three metaphors:

- They turned their backs like a stubborn animal who refuses a yoke.
- They stopped their ears so they could not hear.
- They made their hearts as hard as flint (a rock that sharpens knives).

They were insubordinate, inattentive, and stone-hearted. They did not care. They were insensitive and uncaring about the plight of the poor in the land. They pursued injustice rather than loving their neighbors. They did not listen because they loved themselves more than their neighbors. Zechariah accused postexilic Judah of pursuing the same interests as preexilic Judah. The people had not changed.

Zechariah summarizes the message of the earlier prophets. It is a classic distillation of Amos (5:24), Hosea (4:1–3, 12:6), Micah (6:8), Isaiah (58:6–8), and Jeremiah (7:5–6). It is a stunning message about social responsibility—two prescriptions and two prohibitions:

- Administer true justice or justice and faithfulness.
- Show mercy (*hesed*) and compassion to one another.
- Do not oppress the marginalized (widow, orphan, alien, or poor).
- Do not devise evil in your hearts against each other.

This language rehearses the theme of social injustice so prominent in the prophetic books. The term "devise evil" is situated in a legal context in Zechariah 8:16–17. Those who were charged with protecting the powerless were abusing their power for their own interests. Justice was perverted. The courts, even the priestly courts, facilitated the mistreatment of widows, orphans, aliens, and the poor. Instead of mercy, compassion, justice, and faithfulness, the people "devise[d] evil" against each other. Instead of loving their neighbors, they exploited them.

This perverted the essence of the Torah. It subverted Israel's own history as an enslaved alien loved by the Lord. Just as God loved Israel as an alien (a marginalized outsider), so Israel was to love the alien (the marginalized; cf. Deut. 10:17–20). This is near the heart of God and embodies the greatest commandment—to love the Lord our God with our whole heart. We love God by loving our neighbor; we love God in our neighbor.

The sins of preexilic Israel continued in postexilic Judah. Had the people not learned their lesson? Did they not remember how angry God was about such injustices? Zechariah reminded them.

Amid their injustice, God did not answer when they called because they did not listen when God called. God turned the tables. Whereas they did not show mercy and compassion to the strangers in their midst, so

God made them strangers by scattering them to lands they did not know. Because Israel mistreated the homeless, they became homeless. Their beautiful land—a garden that God had prepared for them—became a desolate region (Jer. 3:19–21).

The message of Zechariah is a word from the Lord: "Return to me, . . . and I will return to you" (Zech. 1:3). But Judah had not yet returned to God. Instead, they continued the practices of their forefathers. They had not heeded the warning or learned the lesson. Judah needed to become a nation for the poor. It needed to become a place of mercy and compassion, of truth and faithfulness, for the underprivileged and powerless.

Would Judah listen? Will we?

QUESTION: What, in Zechariah's message, do we need to hear today?

PRAYER: *Remind us, O God, of your mercy and justice that we might show mercy and practice justice in our own lives.*

THE PROPHETS ENVISION A NEW DAY

TEXT: MALACHI 3:1–2

See, I am sending my messenger to prepare the way before me, and the Lord whom you seek will suddenly come to his temple. The messenger of the covenant in whom you delight—indeed, he is coming, says the LORD *of hosts. But who can endure the day of his coming, and who can stand when he appears?*

In our English Bibles, the last prophet in the Hebrew Bible is Malachi, whose name means *my messenger*. God sent Malachi to a small community of Jews who lived under Persian rule in the area around Jerusalem. Though Judah had returned from Babylonian exile, they had not experienced a national restoration. It seemed like the promises of God had failed. They doubted the love of God. They wondered about God's faithfulness because they were still, essentially, an exiled people living under the oppression and occupation of a hostile empire.

But Malachi envisioned a new day, a time when God would return to the temple (Mal. 3:1). Before God returned, God would send a messenger to prepare the way for the coming of the Lord. Malachi named the messenger: the prophet Elijah (Mal. 4:5).

Malachi prophesied that Elijah would turn Israel's hearts back to God. He would call them to repent. Many of the practices which precipitated the exile continued in Judah. For example, the messenger would confront Judah's sexual immorality, false witnessing, economic injustice (they did not pay just wages), and social injustice against widows, orphans, and aliens in the land (Mal. 3:5).

God fully intended to restore Israel and renew the covenant with them. But before that new day dawned, God would call them to repent by sending a messenger to prepare their hearts for the coming of the Lord, the coming of God's anointed, the Messiah.

At the beginning of the first century, Elijah showed up. We know him as John the Baptizer. In effect, John announced the coming end of the exile. The Lord was coming, and God was carving out a path through the wilderness, as every mountain was made low and every valley was filled in order to make a straight path from Babylonian exile to the restoration of Israel in Jerusalem.

John was a new Elijah and called the people to repent. They wanted to know what they should do, and John's message in Luke 3 is an economic and social one. Whoever has more than they need should share with others. Whoever administers government policy should treat people fairly and not charge more than necessary. Whoever has political or police power should not extort anyone or make false accusations.

Many responded. They confessed their sins, turned from their old ways of life, and were baptized in water for the forgiveness of their sins. Through repentance, confession, and baptism in water, John prepared a people for the coming of the Messiah.

John gathered a group of disciples who were committed to a renewed ethical vision. They were committed to the coming reign of God, and they waited for the Messiah who would come to the temple.

The restoration of Israel is about to begin, the exile is about to end, and the Messiah will soon show up. The story of God, the theodrama, is about to explode with fresh meaning.

QUESTION: How might we prepare for the coming of the reign of God in our own time?

PRAYER: *Lord, we repent of our sins, we regret our mistakes, and we seek your kingdom.*

ACT THREE

MESSIAH

GOD SENDS THE SON AND THE SPIRIT

TEXT: GALATIANS 4:4–7

But when the fullness of time had come, God sent his Son, born of a woman, born under the law, in order to redeem those who were under the law, so that we might receive adoption as children. And because you are children, God has sent the Spirit of his Son into our hearts, crying, "Abba! Father!" So you are no longer a slave but a child, and if a child then also an heir, through God.

As Malachi prophesied and John the Baptizer proclaimed, the Lord was coming. The God who created the world and chose Israel from among the nations was about to come to the temple in order to cleanse it and renew covenant with Israel.

But what does it mean to say that God is coming to the temple? When Jesus the Messiah arrived, cleansed the temple, and gave his body and blood to renew covenant with Israel, how was this the arrival of God at the temple?

Christians confess that the one God is three persons. Christians did not begin describing God as three because they were fond of the number. Instead, when they experienced God in Jesus and through the Holy Spirit, they named the one God as three: Father, Son, and Spirit.

The God of Israel is one God, and there is only one God. Israel confessed this monotheistic faith through the Shema: "Hear, O Israel: The Lord is our God, the Lord alone" (Deut. 6:4). When the apostle Paul unpacked this confession, he named the Father as the one God and the Son as the one Lord (1 Cor. 8:6). As Christians gave a new interpretation to Israel's Shema, they affirmed God's community as well as unity. We see this play out in the theodrama.

The drama is nicely summarized in Galatians 4:4–6. In the fullness of time, when God was ready to come to the temple to cleanse it and renew life with Israel, God sent the Son. He was born of a woman as truly human and born under the law as a descendant of Abraham in order to redeem the world. God became human to suffer for all, and he was born a Jew to extend the inheritance of Israel to all nations. As a descendant of Abraham, the Son became the means by which Gentiles would become children of God and inherit the promise of Abraham.

Just as Israel enjoyed the presence of God at the temple, so every child of God by faith in Jesus is also gifted with God's presence. God has sent the Holy Spirit into the hearts of believers. Living in our hearts, the Spirit cries, "Abba." As children of God, we—both Jew and Gentile—are no longer enslaved to sin but free from its guilt and power. The presence of the Spirit assures us that we are fellow heirs with Christ, heirs of the promise to Abraham.

The Creator God, the God of Israel, in the fullness of time, sent the Son, through whom God created the world, into the world for the sake of the world, and then sent the Holy Spirit into the hearts of believers to secure intimacy with us. The Creator sent the Son, and then, through the Son, sent the Spirit.

This is what Christians call Trinity: Father, Son, and Holy Spirit. We are baptized into the name of the Father, Son, and Spirit (Matt. 28:19), and we have access to the Father through the Son in the Spirit (Eph. 2:18). This one God, who is Father, Son, and Spirit, is the same one who began the theodrama, participates in the theodrama, and will bring it to its completion. The Father, Son, and Spirit, who are the one God, are the main actors in the rest of the story.

QUESTION: What role does each person of the Trinity play in the work of redemption for the sake of the world?

PRAYER: *Glory to the Father, and to the Son, and to the Holy Spirit as it was in the beginning, is now, and will be forever worlds without end. Amen.*

GOD BECOMES A HUMAN BEING

TEXT: JOHN 1:1–2, 14

In the beginning was the Word, and the Word was with God, and the Word was God. He was in the beginning with God. . . . And the Word became flesh and lived among us, and we have seen his glory, the glory as of a father's only son, full of grace and truth.

When God decided to come to the temple and renew covenant with Israel, God came as a human being rather than as a burning bush or an angel. God came in the flesh rather than as a temporary theophany like God's appearance to Israel in the fire and the cloud. God did not come to the temple in some kind of spiritual or celestial form, but in the flesh.

God could have simply created a fully mature human body and united with it, but God intended to fully live out a human life. Rather than dropping out of the sky as a fully developed human, God was born, grew, matured, and eventually died. In other words, God intended to fully experience human life from birth to death.

Therefore, the Creator sent the Son, the one through whom God created the world, into the world, and the Son became human through birth, born of a woman named Mary by the power of the Spirit. Ever since, generations have called Mary, blessed and favored by God, as the one through whom the Son of God became flesh and entered the world.

This was the Trinity in action. The Creator sent the Son, the Son entered the virgin womb of Mary, and the Spirit was the means by which Mary conceived and gave birth to a human child, who is called the Son of the Most High. This child was both the son of Mary and the Son of God, both human and divine. God became flesh through a woman named Mary.

This does not mean that Jesus was half God and half human. On the contrary, the Son who was fully God and the instrument of creation itself became flesh and, as flesh, grew into the fullness of human life. God became fully human without ceasing to be God. In this way, God identifies with us.

Through full immersion into the human condition as a human being, God learned to empathize with us. When God became one of us, God fully experienced what it meant to be human, to feel like a human, to struggle as a human, and to experience the limitations all human beings share.

When God became flesh, God chose self-limitation. God, in the person of the Son, lived in a body that was limited by time and space. The Son lived in Galilee and Judea, not in North America. The Son lived in a specific time when Roman emperors oppressed the Mediterranean world. The Son learned what it meant to grow from infancy to childhood and from childhood to adulthood. The Son grew in wisdom and in years. The Son, as a human being, grew and developed like any other human being.

We know this human being as Jesus, born of Mary, raised in Nazareth, and the cousin of John the Baptizer. The two, Jesus and John, would meet in the baptismal waters of the Jordan River.

QUESTION: What is the significance of saying Jesus experienced the world just like we experience it—that is, from a limited, developing, and maturing perspective?

PRAYER: *O God, we confess that you became human, and nothing is more astounding than that!*

WHY DID GOD BECOME HUMAN?

TEXT: HEBREWS 2:14–18

Since, therefore, the children share flesh and blood, he himself likewise shared the same things, so that through death he might destroy the one who has the power of death, that is, the devil, and free those who all their lives were held in slavery by the fear of death. For it is clear that he did not come to help angels, but the descendants of Abraham. Therefore he had to become like his brothers and sisters in every respect, so that he might be a merciful and faithful high priest in the service of God, to make a sacrifice of atonement for the sins of the people. Because he himself was tested by what he suffered, he is able to help those who are being tested.

One of the most foundational and wondrous confessions of the Christian faith is this: in the birth of Jesus, God became a human being. The birth of Jesus was the incarnation of God. God became flesh through the womb of Mary. This lies at the heart of Christianity, and it is the story of God's humility and love.

So, why did God become human?

God became one of us to participate in material creation as a creature, and through this participation, God affirmed, redeemed, and sanctified creation. Becoming flesh, living in his own skin, and being raised from the dead in a glorified human body testify to God's goal for creation itself. The incarnation of God and the resurrection of Jesus attest to God's love for the creation and the divine intent to make all things new, including the creation.

God became one of us in order to unite God and humanity. Human beings were created in the image of God. Therefore, there is an embedded similarity between God and humanity. While the union brings together the infinite and the finite, humanity was created to be like God and share in the communion of the triune God. The incarnation is the actual union of God and humanity in the person of the Son, and through that union, God and humanity share life together in wondrous intimacy through the communion of the Holy Spirit.

God became one of us in order to reveal God to us. The life of Jesus tells the story of how God would act as a human being. In Jesus, we see who God is, how God behaves, and how God relates to people. We see God when we see Jesus. In this sense, Jesus is the truth, God in the flesh. We know God because we know Jesus.

God became one of us in order to experience and empathize with our suffering. God in God's own essence does not know what it is like to be thirsty, to be hungry, or to experience physical pain and temptation. God in Jesus, however, experienced all of these human frailties. In this way, God becomes fully empathetic through Jesus. God in Jesus shares our pain and temptations, sits on the mourner's bench with us, and dies with us. God fully knows us—not just cognitively, but also existentially and experientially.

God became one of us in order to redeem us through the sacrifice of God's own life in Jesus. As God and as a human, Jesus is the mediator between God and humanity. God became human so that, as a human being, God might suffer death as an act of divine self-substitution. God, as human, experienced the wounds and stripes of our sin. In this way, Jesus, as God in the flesh, engaged the powers of evil and defeated them through his obedience.

The incarnation is not simply a necessary condition for the cross. It is much more. Through the incarnation, God becomes part of the creation, unites God and humanity in the person of Jesus, reveals God's identity, empathizes with our suffering, and redeems us through the cross.

God in the flesh is the heart of Christianity, and without it, there is no Christianity but simply another prophetic movement in a long line of other religious agendas throughout history. God in the flesh means that God loves us, empathizes with us, and redeems us as a fellow human being and fellow sufferer. That is why we confess that Jesus is God.

QUESTION: Which of the reasons given above are most significant to you and most impact your life with God?

PRAYER: *Why, O God, would you become human except to love us more deeply and know us more profoundly? Thank you!*

THE MESSIAH IS IMMERSED WITH ISRAEL

TEXT: LUKE 3:21–22

Now when all the people were baptized, and when Jesus also had been baptized and was praying, the heaven was opened, and the Holy Spirit descended upon him in bodily form like a dove. And a voice came from heaven, "You are my Son, the Beloved; with you I am well pleased."

God sent John the Baptizer to prepare Israel to receive their Messiah. John called Israel to repent and invited them into the water of repentance. They came to the water confessing their sins, turning from their sins, and submitting to baptism for the forgiveness of sins.

Jesus, Israel's Messiah, was also baptized by John.

This is startling. Jesus submitted to a ritual designed for sinners. But perhaps it is not so startling. Jesus ultimately died a death designed for sinners. Jesus was numbered with the transgressors, both in his death and baptism. Through baptism, Jesus joined sinners in the water just as he would later share a cross with them.

More specifically, Jesus identified with Israel. He submitted to God's command as part of faithful Israel. Jesus joined other obedient believers in submitting to God's requirement as preparation for the coming kingdom in anticipation of the coming end to the exile. In his baptism, Jesus represented Israel, just as he did on the cross.

There is more. Jesus was anointed by the Holy Spirit. God tore open the heavens, and the Spirit descended upon Jesus as a dove. In this way, God came to Israel once again. God poured the Spirit upon Jesus, and this was the beginning of God's renewed kingdom presence in the world. When Jesus received the Spirit, this anticipated the future moment when God would pour the Spirit on all flesh at Pentecost. The Spirit empowered the Messiah for his ministry. Just as Israel crossed the Red Sea and enjoyed the descent of God into the tabernacle, so Jesus came up out of the water and the Holy Spirit descended upon him and anointed him as Israel's Messiah.

God affirmed Jesus at his baptism. God said, "You are my Son, the Beloved; with you I am well pleased" (Luke 3:22). After Jesus came out of the water, God loved the Son, poured the Spirit on him, and spoke over him. God used this same language to describe Israel in Psalms and Isaiah. The Messiah was Israel's faithful remnant and the representative of Israel. The baptism of Jesus was a new beginning for Israel. It was a new crossing of the Red Sea, a new liberation. Just as this language belonged to Israel, so it also belongs to those who believe in Jesus.

We enter this same story through our baptism.

Just as Jesus was immersed in water, the Spirit was poured on him, and God affirmed him; that is our baptism, too! When we are baptized, God pours the Spirit on us and we, too, are anointed. When we are baptized, God says over us, "This is my child." When we are baptized, God delights in us and rejoices over us. In our baptism, just as in Jesus's baptism, the Trinity is at work: God loves us in the Son and anoints us with the Spirit.

The baptism of Jesus is our model. Jesus invites us to follow him, and if we are disciples of Jesus, we will follow him into the water and experience God's gracious delight and gifts. It is an act of obedient discipleship, but it is also a moment when God acts. God delights in us, God declares us the children of God, God anoints with the Spirit, and God forgives our sins.

QUESTION: Why was Jesus baptized, and what does this say about your own baptism?

PRAYER: *We love you, O God, because you first loved us.*

THE MESSIAH GOES INTO THE WILDERNESS WITH ISRAEL

TEXT: LUKE 4:1–2A

Jesus, full of the Holy Spirit, returned from the Jordan and was led by the Spirit in the wilderness, where for forty days he was tempted by the devil.

Rising from the waters of baptism, Jesus was anointed with the Holy Spirit. God affirmed him, loved him, and expressed pure delight with him. And then, immediately, the Spirit threw him into the wilderness (Mark 1:12).

No waiting. No downtime. No pampering. Jesus was immediately sequestered away in a wilderness boot camp. The Spirit of God drove him into the wilderness and led him while he was in the wilderness. Once again, we see the Trinity at work: God sent the Son into the wilderness by the Spirit.

Why did the Spirit throw Jesus into the wilderness? Jesus passed through the water, just as Israel passed through the sea. Just as they spent forty years in the Sinai wilderness, so Jesus spent forty days in the Judean wilderness. Jesus was reliving the history of Israel.

Deuteronomy 8 provides insight into the meaning of the wilderness for Israel. Jesus himself quotes from that chapter. Deuteronomy describes the wilderness as a place where God humbled and discipled Israel. God's firstborn among the nations was tested to reveal what was in their hearts. They were humbled in their dependence upon God. They were spiritually formed by their wilderness experience.

This, in part, is the meaning of the wilderness for Jesus as well as for us. Jesus was tested in a hostile environment—Satan was there. Jesus was tested, humbled, and discipled in the wilderness. Yet, the Spirit of God was there, too. Jesus was not alone—God was with him.

The same is true for us. The wilderness comes in many forms—depression, grief, loneliness, persecution, injustice, and sickness. While those come to us without our consent, sometimes we also choose the wilderness as a place to know God more fully and more deeply. God is present in the wilderness. The wilderness tests us in order to reveal our hearts, it humbles us as we recognize our powerlessness and dependency on God, and it disciples us as it trains us for the mission of God.

The wilderness revealed Israel's identity and formed them as the people of God. In the same way, Jesus affirmed his identity in the wilderness. He chose the way of the cross instead of the consumerist path of wealth and power. Jesus refused the offers of Satan and submitted to the path God had set before him.

We are not abandoned in the wilderness. Israel was not left alone as God journeyed with them. Jesus was not alone as angels ministered to him and the Spirit rested upon him. Angels and the Spirit minister to us as well (cf. Heb. 1:14). God is present with us in the wilderness. That presence strengthens and empowers us to not only endure it but to be formed by it.

The wilderness story of Israel is also Jesus's story, and Jesus's story is our story. Just as we followed Jesus into the water, so we follow him into the wilderness. Or, perhaps, like Jesus, God will sometimes throw us into the wilderness. Whatever the case, God will be there, too. And, through the wilderness experience, God will form us into the image of Jesus.

QUESTION: Why did God send Jesus into the wilderness? What did Jesus gain from that experience?

PRAYER: *We do not live by bread alone, O God; we live by your every word.*

THE MESSIAH BEGINS HIS MINISTRY

TEXT: MATTHEW 4:13–17

He left Nazareth and made his home in Capernaum by the sea, in the territory of Zebulun and Naphtali, so that what had been spoken through the prophet Isaiah might be fulfilled:

"Land of Zebulun, land of Naphtali,
on the road by the sea, across the Jordan, Galilee of the Gentiles—
the people who sat in darkness
have seen a great light,
and for those who sat in the region and shadow of death
light has dawned."

From that time Jesus began to proclaim, "Repent, for the kingdom of heaven has come near."

Jesus went into the water to be baptized, then he was thrown into the wilderness, and finally he went into Galilee.

In each movement, Jesus relived the story of Israel. Jesus went through the water just as Israel did in their exodus from Egypt. Jesus went into the wilderness, just as Israel did for forty years. Jesus entered Galilee with hope and promise, just as Israel entered the promised land in the time of Joshua.

The ministry of Jesus continued the ministry of Israel. Just as Israel was a witness to the presence of God in the world as a light to the nations, so Jesus renewed that mission by serving Israel and ultimately sending his disciples to the nations. Israel came out of the wilderness to minister among the nations, and Jesus came out of the wilderness to minister in Israel as he prepared a people to serve the nations.

Indeed, disciples followed Jesus into the water, followed Jesus into the wilderness, and embraced the mission of Jesus as their own.

Coming out of the wilderness, Jesus heralded the good news of God, the gospel of God. But what was this good news?

The Gospel of Mark begins with this line: "The beginning of the good news of Jesus Christ, the Son of God" (Mark 1:1). Mark's Gospel narrates and tells the story of the gospel, the good news. It is about Jesus.

Mark 1:15 specifies the good news. When Jesus heralded the good news of God, he preached this simple message. "The kingdom of God has come near." This was the time of God's visitation; the time of God's in-breaking. The reign of God was coming. "The time is fulfilled." It is now.

As we walk through the ministry of Jesus, we will see more clearly what the "kingdom of God" is and how its appearance is good news. Simply put, the reign of God arrives in the ministry of Jesus in the midst of a violent and evil age. God's justice will set things right, God's mercy will heal the wounded, and God's peace will reign in the world. This comes in the person of Jesus, who embodies the reign of God.

This good news invites a response: Repent and believe, Jesus says, or reform and declare your allegiance. Like John the Baptizer, Jesus called Israel to repent. The people must align themselves with the purposes of the gospel, the reign of God, through repentance and reformation of life. Penitent, they committed to the good news of the kingdom, and they cast their allegiance to the coming reign of God.

This is a call for the church as well. Just as we followed Jesus into the water and into the wilderness, so we follow him into his ministry. We, too, herald the coming of the kingdom of God. We follow Jesus by heralding the good news and practicing the good news in our lives.

Coming from the water and out of the wilderness, Jesus communicated his central message: "The kingdom of God has come near;

repent, and believe the good news" (Mark 1:15). This is the heartbeat of the theodrama.

QUESTION: Why is the coming of the reign of God "good news"?

PRAYER: *We repent, O God, and we believe the good news!*

THE MESSIAH MINISTERS TO ISRAEL

TEXT: LUKE 4:16–21

When he came to Nazareth, where he had been brought up, he went to the synagogue on the sabbath day, as was his custom. He stood up to read, and the scroll of the prophet Isaiah was given to him. He unrolled the scroll and found the place where it was written:

"The Spirit of the Lord is upon me,
because he has anointed me
to bring good news to the poor.
He has sent me to proclaim release to the captives
and recovery of sight to the blind,
to let the oppressed go free,
to proclaim the year of the Lord's favor."

And he rolled up the scroll, gave it back to the attendant, and sat down. The eyes of all in the synagogue were fixed on him. Then he began to say to them, "Today this scripture has been fulfilled in your hearing."

Coming out of the wilderness and entering into Galilee, Jesus, filled with the Spirit, began to teach and heal the sick. He returned to the synagogue in Nazareth to introduce his messianic mission to his hometown.

Unrolling the scroll, he found the place in Isaiah 61 and read it (Luke 4:18–19). The Spirit had anointed him to preach good news to the poor. The Spirit had empowered him to liberate people from their oppression, diseases, and enslavement. The ministry of Jesus was a Jubilee year.

Rolling the scroll back up and handing it to the attendant, Jesus boldly declared: "Today this scripture has been fulfilled in your hearing."

Isaiah's message described the mission of Jesus. He was God's anointed, and his messianic mission was to bring "good news," or the gospel, to the poor, the prisoners, the blind, and the oppressed. His mission had economic, social, and spiritual implications. Through Jesus, God would liberate all who were enslaved by the present evil age. It was a time of divine favor and grace.

In the language of Israel, it was Jubilee! What Jubilee should have meant to Israel throughout its history broke into the world through the ministry of Jesus. Jubilee means that prisoners are released, the poor get good news through debt release, the sick are healed, sins are forgiven, and the oppressed are liberated from their bondage. Jubilee had arrived in the person of Jesus, who proclaimed the reign of God had come near.

At a "big-picture" level, from the viewpoint of the whole theodrama, Jubilee reverses the curse. What I mean by curse is what I think Revelation 22:3 means when it says that there will be no more curse in the new heaven and new Earth. The curse is whatever enslaves the creation and its people. The curse fills creation with mourning, pain, injustice, poverty, evil, and, ultimately, death.

The mission of Jesus was to reverse the curse. The ministry of Jesus liberated humanity from the curse. This was the mission of Jesus. It is why he was sent. It was what he preached and what he did.

This is the "good news of the kingdom of God" (Luke 4:43). The kingdom of God has come near, and when the kingdom comes near, the brokenness of the world is healed. The curse is reversed.

The kingdom is not the structures and organization of an institutionalized church. Rather, the kingdom is the reign of God in the world. When God reigns, there is no more curse. When God reigns, people are reconciled. When God reigns, diseases, demons, and death are overcome. When God reigns, sins are forgiven. When God reigns, the poor and the oppressed get justice. That is good news. That is the gospel!

QUESTION: What is the mission of Jesus?

PRAYER: *May your mission, O God, become our mission!*

SEEKING FIRST THE KINGDOM OF GOD AND ITS RIGHTEOUSNESS

TEXT: MATTHEW 6:33

But strive first for the kingdom of God and his righteousness, and all these things will be given to you as well.

The Sermon on the Mount (Matt. 5–7) is the epitome of kingdom ethics and discipleship.

The sermon opens with the beatitudes, which begin and end with a promise that the blessed belong to the kingdom of heaven (Matt. 5:3, 10). The sermon ends with a promise that those who "do the will of [the] Father" will "enter the kingdom of heaven" (Matt. 7:21). At the heart of the sermon is the call to "strive first for the kingdom and his righteousness" (Matt. 6:33).

The kingdom of God is the priority for disciples of Jesus. Their whole lives are oriented toward the embrace of and participation in the kingdom of God. Nothing shapes their lives other than the reality of God's reign in the world.

This is a lofty goal, and it is difficult to practice. Worries about food, clothing, and shelter often displace this commitment. Religious practices of fasting, prayer, and the giving of alms often become a substitute for it. We externalize our obedience by avoiding murder, adultery, oath breaking, and vengeance instead of rooting out anger, lust, dishonesty, and hate. We find it easier to project righteousness through external means rather than embrace righteousness in both body and soul.

This is why Jesus said that the righteousness of those who would "enter the kingdom of heaven" must exceed "that of the scribes and Pharisees" (Matt. 5:20). The disciples of Jesus practice Torah, but not only on the surface. Rather, the meaning of the Torah reaches deep into their souls and transforms anger into forgiveness, lust into faithfulness to and love for spouse, dishonesty into integrity and oath keeping, and hate into a love for enemy.

Seeking the righteousness of the kingdom of God is to seek to become like God. This is the essence of a kingdom ethic; it is the essence of the Torah. The law and the prophets are built on a profound commitment to treat others like we would like to be treated.

This is what it means to do the will of God. It is not primarily found in miracle working, prophesying, or casting out demons. It is found in the ethic of the kingdom of God. It is found in embodying the righteousness of God outlined in the Sermon on the Mount through love, devotion, and obedience.

This is the one who builds on a rock. When we hear the words of Jesus and practice them, then we are like a house with a solid foundation that will not collapse when the storms come.

In the midst of the storms, disciples of Jesus seek first the kingdom of God, and the promise is that God will supply all that is needed. This commitment dispels worry, anxiety, and fear because disciples are confident that God will provide. Our focus is on the kingdom of God and its righteousness.

QUESTION: Why is externalizing righteousness so much easier than internalizing it?

PRAYER: *Pour out your Spirit upon us, dear Father, that we might practice the words of your Son.*

PLEDGING ALLEGIANCE TO THE MESSIAH'S KINGDOM

TEXT: MATTHEW 6:9–13

"Pray then in this way:
Our Father in heaven,
hallowed be your name.
Your kingdom come.
Your will be done,
on earth as it is in heaven.
Give us this day our daily bread.
And forgive us our debts,
as we also have forgiven our debtors.
And do not bring us to the time of trial,
but rescue us from the evil one."

Near the middle of the Sermon on the Mount, Jesus provided a model prayer for kingdom people. Some call it the Lord's Prayer or the "Our Father." From at least the late first century, some disciples of Jesus have prayed this prayer three times a day (Didache 8:2–3). As a daily prayer, it functions both as a petition for God's care and a daily pledge of allegiance.

In the prayer, we address the Creator as one who is both intimate in relationship with us and transcendent beyond us. The Creator is "our Father in heaven" (Matt. 6:9).

In the first half of the prayer, we commit ourselves to the transcendent God. We pledge allegiance to the divine name, will, and kingdom. We have no other allegiance. This is the heart of worship itself—a loyalty that transcends everything else in our lives and orders the whole of our lives under God's reign. Anything else is idolatry. We call upon God to act so as to sanctify God's name, accomplish God's will, and bring the divine kingdom to the Earth.

As we ask the Creator to enact the divine agenda, we also commit ourselves to become the instruments of that work. We pray for the sanctification of the name, the accomplishment of the will, and the in-breaking of the kingdom, but our prayer is no mere passive wait. Instead, we pursue those goals as proactive agents of the name, will, and reign of God. Empowered by God, we commit to cooperate with God to bring heaven to Earth.

To pray this prayer is to subordinate our agendas and desires to God's kingdom. We acknowledge that God's will rather than our own is primary. We pledge allegiance to God's kingdom above the kingdoms of this world. We seek the will of God.

The prayer, however, is not simply about our allegiance to God; it is also a testimony of God's commitment (yes, even allegiance) to us. God is present with us in our daily lives. The last three petitions assume God's benevolence for us. They claim God's promises of daily sustenance, reconciliation (forgiveness), and power against the evil one. God is for us, and God will not abandon us.

God feeds us, forgives us, and protects us. We need the divine gift of life (physical, emotional, spiritual), and we need the divine power that overcomes the evil one. When we pray the Lord's Prayer, God's promise is renewed in our lives—God will sustain us in all our needs, whether they concern bread, sin, or spiritual warfare.

At the same time, when we receive these gifts, we are also obliged to share them with others. When we pray for bread, we commit to share the bread God gives. When we pray for forgiveness, we commit to forgive others. When we pray for protection, we commit to protect others.

The Lord's Prayer, prayed daily with purpose and commitment, will transform us. Through this prayer, we acknowledge God's transcendence, commit ourselves to God's agenda, and embrace a new way of living in the world that conforms to God's will, honors God's name, and manifests God's reign. Through this prayer, we trust in God's daily provision for our lives, receive God's forgiveness as we forgive others, and embrace God's protection against the evil one.

Through this prayer, we pledge our allegiance to God, and we remember God's pledge to us.

QUESTION: Which petition in the Lord's Prayer is most significant for you in this moment in your life?

PRAYER: *Your kingdom come, O God, your will be done on Earth as it is in heaven.*

DID JESUS PREACH THE GOSPEL?

TEXT: LUKE 4:40–43

As the sun was setting, all those who had any who were sick with various kinds of diseases brought them to him; and he laid his hands on each of them and cured them. Demons also came out of many, shouting, "You are the Son of God!" But he rebuked them and would not allow them to speak, because they knew that he was the Messiah. At daybreak he departed and went into a deserted place. And the crowds were looking for him; and when they reached him, they wanted to prevent him from leaving them. But he said to them, "I must proclaim the good news of the kingdom of God to the other cities also; for I was sent for this purpose."

Did Jesus preach the gospel? Yes and no. It depends on what one means by "gospel."

For many, the gospel is the death and resurrection of Jesus. If that is what we mean by gospel, then Jesus did not publicly preach the gospel. It was only in the last months of the third year of his ministry that Jesus even talked about his death and resurrection, and then it was only with his closest disciples (Matt. 16; Luke 9; Mark 9).

But, according to the Gospels, Jesus did preach the gospel; that is, Jesus preached the good news of the kingdom of God (Matt. 4:23, 9:35; Luke 4:43, 8:1; or "good news of God" in Mark 1:14–15). Indeed, his messianic mission was "to preach the gospel to the poor" (Matt. 11:5; Luke 4:18, 7:22).

But if the gospel in the Gospels is not the death and resurrection of Jesus, what is the "good news of the kingdom of God" (Luke 4:43)? It announces that the kingdom is coming, the kingdom of God has come near, and the reign of God is breaking into the world to transform it. The good news of the kingdom is that heaven is coming to Earth.

When the kingdom comes, people are reconciled to God, the blind see, the lame walk, the dead are raised, the marginalized are included, the oppressed are liberated, and sins are forgiven. The good news of the kingdom is the arrival of heaven such that the will of God is done on Earth just as it is in heaven. This is the good news, or the gospel, that Jesus announced.

Some think social action or reconciliation among human beings is the epitome of kingdom work, and others stress the forgiveness of sins or reconciliation with God as the fundamental proclamation of the church. The ministry of Jesus models both/and rather than either/or. The following examples from the Gospels illustrate how it is both/and.

> Matthew 4:23 (NIV): "Jesus went throughout Galilee, teaching in their synagogues, proclaiming the good news of the kingdom, and healing every disease and sickness among the people."
>
> Matthew 10:7–8: "As you go, proclaim the good news: 'The kingdom of heaven has come near.' Cure the sick, raise the dead, cleanse the lepers, cast out demons."
>
> Luke 9:2, 6: "He sent them out to proclaim the kingdom of God and heal. . . . They departed and went through the villages, bringing the good news and curing diseases everywhere."

Kingdom ministry heals the sick and reconciles people to God and each other. The proclamation of the kingdom of God identifies those gifts as the good news of the kingdom of God.

Did Jesus preach the gospel? Yes, he did! He preached the good news of the kingdom of God. But Jesus not only preached the gospel; he also enacted the gospel. He healed diseases, raised the dead, drove out demons, reconciled people, forgave sin, and included the marginalized.

This is the essence of the message and ministry of Jesus, and it is our ministry, too.

QUESTION: Did Jesus preach the gospel? What is the gospel?

PRAYER: *We praise you, O God, for the year of Jubilee!*

THE MESSIAH CONFRONTS THE REIGN OF SATAN

TEXT: LUKE 10:17–20

The seventy returned with joy, saying, "Lord, in your name even the demons submit to us!" He said to them, "I watched Satan fall from heaven like a flash of lightning. See, I have given you authority to tread on snakes and scorpions, and over all the power of the enemy; and nothing will hurt you. Nevertheless, do not rejoice at this, that the spirits submit to you, but rejoice that your names are written in heaven."

Jesus did not pursue his ministry alone. He discipled twelve apostles, and he also sent seventy disciples into surrounding villages to further the messianic mission.

When Jesus sent out the seventy, he told them to proclaim the good news of the kingdom ("Cure the sick who are there, and say to them, 'The kingdom of God has come near to you'" [Luke 10:9]).

During his ministry, Jesus called others alongside him to participate in the mission of God, and Jesus still calls disciples to continue his ministry. Just as Jesus declared the message that the "kingdom of God is near" (the "good news of the kingdom" Luke 4:43) and healed the sick (reversing the curse), his disciples followed him into the world to announce the nearness of the kingdom and to participate in the reversal of the curse. Disciples proclaimed the good news of the kingdom and healed the sick.

Healing the sick is one example of the presence of the kingdom. Healers, doctors, nurses, and medical professionals are instruments of the kingdom of God. Environmental scientists, who protect and nurture the environment, are also instruments. Educators, who dispel ignorance and equip students for responsible living, are instruments of the kingdom of God. Social workers, who seek justice for the oppressed and neglected, are instruments of the kingdom of God. The list could go on and on. All disciples announce the good news of the forgiveness of sins and reconciliation with God, and disciples also make disciples.

At the same time, as disciples of Jesus, our careers should serve the ends of the kingdom of God. We do not pursue our careers for the sake of money, greed, and power. Instead, our vocations—whether in medicine, law, education, or service industries—serve the kingdom of God for the sake of the world. Disciples recognize this as part of the good news of the kingdom. Disciples proclaim the reality of God through their careers, and by those careers, they enact the good news of the kingdom. They announce the forgiveness of sins and seek to make more disciples.

When the disciples returned, excited by their success, Jesus celebrated their joy by saying, "I watched Satan fall from heaven like a flash of lightning" (Luke 10:18).

When the curse is reversed—that is, when the poor receive good news, the blind see, the oppressed receive justice, sinners are forgiven, people groups are reconciled, and prisoners are released—Satan falls. Satan is crushed by the heel of the kingdom of God. Satan falls every time the kingdom breaks into the world, whether in the forgiveness of sins, reconciliation among people groups, healing of the sick, or liberation of the oppressed. Satan falls whenever and wherever the curse is reversed.

Disciples of Jesus know their mission is about reconciliation—the reconciliation of God with humanity, the reconciliation of people groups within humanity, and the reconciliation of humanity with the creation. The mission of Jesus is about how the kingdom of God breaks into the present to reverse the curse and renew blessing—to heal and bless all nations. Every victory anticipates the future. Every victory is a promise of the future. Satan is falling, and that is good news.

QUESTION: Name some moments and times in your life or in the lives of others when you have seen Satan fall.

PRAYER: *May your kingdom, O God, defeat the reign of darkness in the world!*

THE MESSIAH BEGINS THE JOURNEY TO THE CROSS

TEXT: LUKE 9:18–22

Once when Jesus was praying alone, with only the disciples near him, he asked them, "Who do the crowds say that I am?" They answered, "John the Baptist; but others, Elijah; and still others, that one of the ancient prophets has arisen." He said to them, "But who do you say that I am?" Peter answered, "The Messiah of God." He sternly ordered and commanded them not to tell anyone, saying, "The Son of Man must undergo great suffering, and be rejected by the elders, chief priests, and scribes, and be killed, and on the third day be raised."

The ministry of Jesus generated widespread speculation about his identity. Was he the resurrected John the Baptizer? Or Elijah? Or another prophet in the long line of prophets? There was no consensus, but many believed God was doing something through Jesus.

Jesus, however, was most interested in what his disciples thought. They had, no doubt, pondered this question many times. At a key moment in the ministry, Jesus, when his face was turned toward Jerusalem and his death, Peter confessed, "You are the Messiah" (Mark 8:29). It was a bold statement, a political statement. It was about the reign of God in the world. God's anointed king was on the Earth. That was dangerous language in the context of imperial Roman occupation, and many claimants to the title had already been executed in the past couple of generations.

Peter's confession was courageous, but Jesus immediately silenced him. The message was too provocative, and the time for Jesus's public witness as Messiah had not yet come. The messianic secret must remain hidden.

At once, however, we see a contrast between Jesus's understanding of his messianic mission and Peter's take on it. Peter saw glory without suffering; perhaps he saw a great military overthrow of Roman oppression and the imminent enthronement of Jesus as king in Jerusalem. If Jesus could command the demons, death, and the chaos of the sea, he could certainly defeat the Romans. Peter's understanding, however, was Satanic. It was the way of violence rather than self-giving love. The political order—the way of sinful humanity—pursues violent means for safety and preservation, but God would secure peace and justice through the suffering of Jesus.

Jesus understood that there could be no glory without suffering. The Son of man, the one who ultimately triumphs over the enemies of God, must first suffer death before he experiences resurrection glory. The reign of God comes through suffering, not military conquest. The cross comes before the crown.

To follow Jesus—to become a disciple—is to deny ourselves and bear a cross. Too often, we trivialize this language and tend to think of the cross as only the symbol of love and reconciliation that it has become in the history of Christianity. But in Roman-occupied Palestine, it was a symbol of horror, pain, and shame. Using the word *cross*, Jesus pointed to the manner of his own death.

Following Jesus involves a willingness to suffer for the sake of the kingdom of God. Following Jesus means taking up a cross—putting that crossbeam on our backs—and dying with Jesus. To take up the cross means to follow Jesus to a cross. If we followed Jesus into the water, we also called to follow him to a cross.

The ministry of Jesus had turned a corner. His disciples confessed him as the Messiah, and Jesus began to tell those disciples that this would mean his suffering and death. They could not fathom that, but Jesus knew what lay ahead. After several years of ministry among the Jews in Galilee, Jesus turned his face toward Jerusalem, where death awaited him.

QUESTION: What does the cross of Jesus represent to you?

PRAYER: *O God, we confess that Jesus is your Messiah, your Son!*

GOD GIVES THE MESSIAH HOPE

TEXT: LUKE 9:28–36A

Now about eight days after these sayings Jesus took with him Peter and John and James, and went up on the mountain to pray. And while he was praying, the appearance of his face changed, and his clothes became dazzling white. Suddenly they saw two men, Moses and Elijah, talking to him. They appeared in glory and were speaking of his departure, which he was about to accomplish at Jerusalem. Now Peter and his companions were weighed down with sleep; but since they had stayed awake, they saw his glory and the two men who stood with him. Just as they were leaving him, Peter said to Jesus, "Master, it is good for us to be here; let us make three dwellings, one for you, one for Moses, and one for Elijah"—not knowing what he said. While he was saying this, a cloud came and overshadowed them; and they were terrified as they entered the cloud. Then from the cloud came a voice that said, "This is my Son, my Chosen; listen to him!" When the voice had spoken, Jesus was found alone.

After the Holy Spirit anointed Jesus at his baptism, the Spirit led him into the wilderness for a period of testing. When the disciples finally confessed Jesus as the Messiah, they were shocked to hear that now Jesus must suffer and die before the glory of the kingdom comes into the world.

At the moment when Jesus turned his face toward Jerusalem and his eventual death, he took three disciples—Peter, James, and John—onto a high mountain to pray. The disciples, however, slept, and ultimately,

Peter said something awkward. These particulars anticipate what would happen in the garden of Gethsemane. Jesus would go there to pray, he would take these same three disciples with him, they would sleep while he prayed, and Peter would say and do something awkward. Jesus climbed this mountain in order to pray and prepare himself for the coming trials that would test his commitment to the mission of God.

But this also became a moment that anticipated his resurrection and ascension into glory. Two figures appeared with Jesus, a cloud appeared, and glory surrounded Jesus. The glory of this transfiguration, this metamorphosis, is the glory of the resurrection, ascension, and the second coming of King Jesus. Suffering, though necessary, was not Jesus's final destiny.

When God transfigured Jesus, the appearance of Jesus changed. Though he presently lived in a mortal, dying body, his transfigured appearance was one of future glory, the glory of the resurrected Christ. This was a proleptic event in the life of Jesus. In other words, it was the experience of his future glory in the present—the experience of the glory of his resurrection, ascension, and future second coming. In answer to his prayer, God encouraged the Son to complete the mission. Jesus was assured that the cross would not be the final act in God's drama, and the grave would not have the last say.

The transfiguration was a foretaste of the future. Though he would suffer, Jesus would rise again. Though the creation, including human bodies, is bound to decay, the resurrection of Jesus promises a different future for the creation. The kingdom of God will, one day, fully come. It came on the Mount of Transfiguration, it came through the Holy Spirit at Pentecost, and it will fully appear when Jesus returns again.

We stand where the disciples stood. We anticipate death, but we hope for glory. We lose our lives in order to save them. We follow Jesus to the cross, and we hope for the resurrection. We give up the whole world in order to follow Jesus that we might gain it in the kingdom of God. We believe in the promise of God, we follow Jesus as his disciples, and we wait with the patience of the Holy Spirit for a new heaven and a new Earth.

His transfiguration promised Jesus a future, and his future is our future. Ultimately, his transfiguration is our transfiguration, as our resurrection bodies will be just like his. Death will not win, and the graves will be emptied. That was the hope of Jesus, and it is our hope as well.

QUESTION: What did the transfiguration mean for Jesus, and what does it mean for his disciples?

PRAYER: *Yes, Lord, we will listen to Jesus, your Son.*

THE MESSIAH IS A SUFFERING SERVANT

TEXT: MARK 10:41–45

When the ten heard this, they began to be angry with James and John. So Jesus called them and said to them, "You know that among the Gentiles those whom they recognize as their rulers lord it over them, and their great ones are tyrants over them. But it is not so among you; but whoever wishes to become great among you must be your servant, and whoever wishes to be first among you must be slave of all. For the Son of Man came not to be served but to serve, and to give his life a ransom for many."

As Jesus and his disciples headed to Jerusalem, he reminded them about what lied ahead. The Son of man would be betrayed, condemned, flogged, humiliated, and executed, though raised from the dead three days later. There must have been an ominous foreboding among the disciples, but their focus was not so much on these future horrendous events as much as it was on their role in the coming reign of the Messiah. They anticipated glory, rank, and power.

James and John approached Jesus with a request. They wanted to sit on the right and left hand of Jesus in his glory. When the kingdom fully arrived, they asked for the highest honors in the kingdom. They asked Jesus for hierarchical power.

But they did not understand what they were asking. Jesus used two metaphors to describe how one becomes great in the kingdom of God.

He asked, "Are you able to drink the cup?" and "be baptized with the baptism that I am baptized with" (Mark 10:38)? Both metaphors point to suffering. Can you drink the cup of suffering and be immersed in it? Jesus, having just told them about his future in Jerusalem, asked if they were willing to suffer as he will suffer. Were they also willing to suffer for Israel?

The request by the two brothers angered the other disciples. They had previously, perhaps on many occasions, argued about who would be the greatest. Despite Jesus's focused teaching about greatness and his exemplary life, the disciples still hungered for rank, power, and status in the coming kingdom.

While the disciples thought of greatness along the lines of Gentile kings who exercised power through status and even violence, this is not the nature of greatness in the kingdom of God. A different sort of power ranking exists in the kingdom of God. It is not rooted in the exercise of power but in service. Greatness is defined by servanthood, not status.

Jesus did not come to reign like Gentile leaders did. Jesus did not come to be served as if others bowed down to his higher rank and catered to his every need. Instead, he came to serve. He came to die as a "ransom for many." The mission of Jesus is to serve, and through this service, Jesus would become great in the kingdom of God.

That kingdom does not call us to greatness through popularity, fame, or even success. The kingdom calls us to greatness through giving and service to others. The one who would be first must become last, and the one who would be great must become the servant of all (Mark 9:35).

This is a difficult lesson to learn. It reverses our violent, self-centered human culture; it reverses the American dream, in which greatness is about success, wealth, and power. But greatness is not found in awards, honors, and pulpits. Instead, it is found in service. Greatness is not defined by how many people hear a lesson from a particular pulpit or watch a particular YouTube video; it is defined by those who visit the prisons, the sick, and the oppressed. Greatness is found in service to the least of these, service to those who are last.

QUESTION: Why is it so difficult to use power and privilege for the sake of the other rather than consuming it for our own sakes?

PRAYER: *Lord, give us the strength to follow you to the cross every day.*

THE MESSIAH COMES TO THE TEMPLE

TEXT: MARK 11:15–18

Then they came to Jerusalem. And he entered the temple and began to drive out those who were selling and those who were buying in the temple, and he overturned the tables of the money changers and the seats of those who sold doves; and he would not allow anyone to carry anything through the temple. He was teaching and saying, "Is it not written,

'My house shall be called a house of prayer for all the nations'?

But you have made it a den of robbers."

And when the chief priests and the scribes heard it, they kept looking for a way to kill him; for they were afraid of him, because the whole crowd was spellbound by his teaching.

Malachi, one of the last of God's messengers to Israel, prophesied that the Lord would come to the temple and judge it. On Palm Sunday, King Jesus, riding on a royal donkey, triumphantly entered Jerusalem. He was hailed as the one who would usher in the kingdom of David. Surrounded by an expectant crowd, he entered the temple, looked at everything, and went home for the evening.

What did Jesus see? The next morning, we find out. The king who came to make peace went to the temple to judge his people. Apparently, he did not like what he had seen the previous day.

He saw "selling and buying," the exchanging of money and the selling of animals in the Court of the Gentiles (Matt. 21:12). This merchandizing, an exploitation of worshipers, profaned the temple courts. Jesus, acting out a prophetic judgment, embodied God's justice by symbolically overturning tables and driving out the animals.

The Gospel of Mark justifies this judgment by quoting Isaiah and Jeremiah. Isaiah 65:7 reminded Israel that the temple is for prayer, including the prayers of the nations. The Court of the Gentiles, where the merchandizing was taking place, diverted the purpose of the court from prayer to economic injustice.

Jeremiah 7:11 accuses the temple authorities of treating the temple like a "den of robbers." In one sense, the temple had become a place for thieves because they defrauded and stole from their neighbors through exploitative practices. In another sense, the temple, as Jeremiah noted, had become a place where injustice hid, a den where robbers hid from judgment. The temple, they thought, could not come under judgment, and, therefore, people were safe in the temple. But they were wrong; the temple would come under judgment, as it had in the past.

The temple authorities understood the implications of this symbolic act. This kingdom act challenged their authority and practices. The kingdom of God judges all other authorities. Because these authorities feared Jesus's popularity and message, they decided he must die in order to preserve their power. Whereas Herodians and Pharisees had conspired to kill Jesus in Galilee (Mark 3:6), the temple authorities in Jerusalem did the same now. Ultimately, together, they would gather a different kind of crowd than the one that cried "Hosanna" (Matt. 21:9) on Palm Sunday. On Good Friday, they would incite a mob to scream, "Crucify him!" (Mark 15:13). The powers of this world, led by the prince of this world, killed Jesus.

God came to the temple and judged it. When Jewish zealots attempted, through violence, to overthrow the Roman occupation and establish their own kingdom, Jerusalem and its magnificent temple fell under the weight of divine judgment.

In the wake of such judgment, how do disciples of Jesus respond? As the Gospel of Mark makes clear in chapter 11, disciples trust God. They pray in faith. They forgive their debtors. In the midst of judgment, disciples live by faith rather than sight, seek reconciliation with others, and pray that God will move mountains.

QUESTION: In what ways has church become a "den of robbers"?

PRAYER: *Give us, O Lord, the courage of Jesus to protest injustices and apply your justice to corrupt institutions.*

THE MESSIAH ESTABLISHES KINGDOM PRIORITIES

TEXT: MARK 12:28–34

One of the scribes came near and heard them disputing with one another, and seeing that he answered them well, he asked him, "Which commandment is the first of all?" Jesus answered, "The first is, 'Hear, O Israel: the Lord our God, the Lord is one; you shall love the Lord your God with all your heart, and with all your soul, and with all your mind, and with all your strength.' The second is this, 'You shall love your neighbor as yourself.' There is no other commandment greater than these." Then the scribe said to him, "You are right, Teacher; you have truly said that 'he is one, and besides him there is no other'; and 'to love him with all the heart, and with all the understanding, and with all the strength,' and 'to love one's neighbor as oneself,'—this is much more important than all whole burnt offerings and sacrifices." When Jesus saw that he answered wisely, he said to him, "You are not far from the kingdom of God." After that no one dared to ask him any question.

As Jesus taught in the temple courts, his opponents confronted him with a series of questions. Jesus enraged the temple authorities when he cleansed the Court of the Gentiles from merchandizers. They questioned his actions and authority. The hostile questions were designed to subvert his popularity or endanger his life.

One scribe was impressed with how well Jesus handled the succession of questions and wondered how Jesus might answer one of the most important questions that rabbis discussed among themselves. He asked, "Which commandment is the first of all?" *Which commandment is the most important one in the Torah?*

Jesus identified two commands in the Torah as the first and second. "Love the Lord your God" is the first, and the second is "love your neighbor." The first comes from Deuteronomy 6:4–5. The second comes from Leviticus 19:18.

What enabled Jesus to so clearly and succinctly identify these two texts as the first and second commandments? Jesus did not read Scripture as a flat text in which every command is as equally important as every other command. Instead, Jesus recognized levels of priority and importance. Some commands are more fundamental than others.

Jesus prioritized these two commands over "burnt offerings and sacrifices." Loving God and neighbor is more important than the temple and its sacrifices. This does not mean sacrifices are unimportant, but there are *more* important commands. The two greatest commands are love God and love neighbor, and we must be careful that we do not make any other command equal in importance.

What makes one more fundamental than another? How are these two imperatives ("love the Lord your God" and "love your neighbor") more important than sacrifices? Perhaps we might see in "love the Lord your God" and "love your neighbor" an act of sacrifice itself. We give ourselves to God (our whole body, soul, and strength) and, in turn, to others. We are the sacrifices. This is more important than any ritual that expresses that devotion.

This reminds us that God loves mercy more than sacrifice (Hosea 6:6) or that what the Lord requires more than a thousand sacrificed rams is "to act justly and to love mercy and to walk humbly with your God" (Mic. 6:8 NIV). We are the sacrifices that God requires (cf. Ps. 40:6–8).

The context in which this exchange took place underscores the importance of "love your neighbor." It appears between the exploitation the money changers practiced in the temple courts (Mark 11:15–16) and Jesus's accusation that wealthy temple authorities exploited widows

(Mark 12:38–40). Jesus identified two examples of economic or social injustice.

Given these temple practices, "love your neighbor" has added significance. It was a further judgment against the temple authorities. The scribe did not ask Jesus for the second commandment. He only inquired about what was "the first of all." Jesus volunteered the second, and the presence of social injustices are a clue as to why. When we love our neighbors, we treat each other fairly, honestly, and with equity, and we oppose all injustices.

The kingdom ethic is to love God and love our neighbor. The kingdom is rooted, grounded, and expressed in love—God's love for us, our love for God, and our love for each other.

When we love God, we love our neighbor. Moreover, we love our neighbor not because we find something worthy of love in our neighbor, but because we love God. The love of God and neighbor are the priorities of the kingdom of God and the driving energy of discipleship. Disciples of Jesus love God first of all, and they love their neighbors as they love their own selves because they love God.

QUESTION: How is loving our neighbor a way of loving God, and what does that look like?

PRAYER: *Instill in our hearts, O God, love both for you and for our neighbors.*

THE MESSIAH SERVES THE TABLE

TEXT: MARK 14:22–25

While they were eating, he took a loaf of bread, and after blessing it he broke it, gave it to them, and said, "Take; this is my body." Then he took a cup, and after giving thanks he gave it to them, and all of them drank from it. He said to them, "This is my blood of the covenant, which is poured out for many. Truly I tell you, I will never again drink of the fruit of the vine until that day when I drink it new in the kingdom of God."

On the evening before his arrest, Jesus reclined at a Passover table with his disciples. Jesus was aware of the conspiracy to kill him. This was Jesus's last meal with his disciples before his death.

"While they were eating," the Gospel of Mark says, Jesus took bread, gave thanks, broke it, and gave it to his disciples. By this, Jesus conformed the breaking of the bread to a Passover meal and, at the same time, gave it a fuller meaning when he said, "This is my body."

Just as the bread of the Passover represents life and liberation, the body of Jesus does the same. Bread is what nourishes life, and the body of the Messiah nourishes believers in their shared life. Eating together, disciples share a community grounded in the gift of the Messiah's body, just as Israel ate with God on Mount Sinai. In effect, Jesus said "my body" will give new life to Israel.

In the same way with the cup, Jesus said, "This is my blood of the covenant, which is poured out for many." Jesus alluded to the sacrificial system of Israel, and the Passover meal gives his words special meaning. The blood of the Lamb gives life. Jesus is the Passover Lamb whose blood renews covenant with Israel.

This language, "blood of the covenant," takes Jewish readers back to Mount Sinai in Exodus 24 when God inaugurated his covenant with Israel and ate with Israel (Exod. 24:8–11). Moreover, Zechariah 9:9–11 suggests that the blood of the covenant frees prisoners; it is liberation. The king who rode into Jerusalem on a donkey was a liberator who "proclaim[s] peace to the nations" (Zech. 9:10 NIV). But King Jesus rode to his death rather than into military action. Jesus liberated through suffering, not violence.

The blood of Jesus is poured out to free the prisoners, to free the enslaved. The suffering servant "poured out his life unto death" and "bore the sin of many" (Isa. 53:12 NIV). Jesus gave life through suffering and dealt with sin through dying. Jesus was the suffering servant of Isaiah who suffered the wounds of exilic Israel and brought new life through his blood. Through his suffering, Jesus ransomed Israel from exile.

The Passover meal now has a new horizon of meaning. While the Passover Lamb died to liberate Israel from Egyptian bondage, Jesus is the true Lamb of God. Through his death, he gives new life and frees us from sin and its power. The original significance of the Passover remains (it still tells the story of Israel), but it is transformed by the new reality that dawns in the death and resurrection of Jesus.

Jesus shared the cup with his disciples. It was the cup of suffering (cf. Mark 10:39–40, 14:36). They drank it that day in solidarity with Jesus as people committed to the way of suffering even though they would shortly falter in that commitment. They drank the cup Jesus drank. But they did not follow Jesus to the cross. We, too, often do the same.

But there is more to this tale; it also bears witness to the reality of the kingdom of God. The next time Jesus ate and drank with his disciples, it would be in that reality. While this includes the future messianic banquet in the new heaven and new Earth, it is also about the in-breaking of the kingdom of God into the present. Jesus is the reality of the kingdom in the world, so the bread and wine are also the reality of the kingdom. In the kingdom of God, Jesus eats and drinks with us. We eat and drink with the living Messiah whose death has transformed life. This calls us to a different kind of life—one that pursues peace and reconciliation rather than violence and estrangement. When we eat and drink together, we recommit ourselves to that way of life.

QUESTION: What do the bread and cup share with those who eat and drink?

PRAYER: *We thank you, O God, for the body and blood of Jesus the Messiah.*

THE MESSIAH AGONIZES OVER DOING THE WILL OF GOD

TEXT: MATTHEW 26:36–46

Then Jesus went with them to a place called Gethsemane; and he said to his disciples, "Sit here while I go over there and pray." He took with him Peter and the two sons of Zebedee, and began to be grieved and agitated. Then he said to them, "I am deeply grieved, even to death; remain here, and stay awake with me." And going a little farther, he threw himself on the ground and prayed, "My Father, if it is possible, let this cup pass from me; yet not what I want but what you want." Then he came to the disciples and found them sleeping; and he said to Peter, "So, could you not stay awake with me one hour? Stay awake and pray that you may not come into the time of trial; the spirit indeed is willing, but the flesh is weak." Again he went away for the second time and prayed, "My Father, if this cannot pass unless I drink it, your will be done." Again he came and found them sleeping, for their eyes were heavy. So leaving them again, he went away and prayed for the third time, saying the same words. Then he came to the disciples and said to them, "Are you still sleeping and taking your rest? See, the hour is at hand, and the Son of Man is betrayed into the hands of sinners. Get up, let us be going. See, my betrayer is at hand."

Leaving the upper room of the Last Supper, Jesus led his disciples across the Kidron Valley onto the Mount of Olives to a place called

Gethsemane. Here Jesus would pray and then suffer betrayal and arrest. That is an answer to prayer none would relish.

Jesus recognized what was coming. The time had come for suffering and death. This strongly contrasts with the prophetic expectations of Zechariah, who said the Mount of Olives would be the place of glory for the Messiah and a moment when the whole Earth would become holy to the Lord. But suffering must come before glory, and Jesus knew this as he entered Gethsemane.

Leaving the majority of the disciples behind, he took Peter, James, and John deeper into the olive trees. These were Jesus's intimates who had shared previous private moments (the transfiguration, for example). Jesus shared with them his deepest emotions. He allowed the three to look into his soul.

He revealed the depth of his angst. As the hour approached, he became deeply disturbed and troubled. His grief was unbearable. He saw no other option than to spend the evening in prayer. Sometimes praying is more important than sleeping. He asked his intimates to keep watch with him while he prayed privately. He hoped they would pray for him, but, alas, they slept.

At least two emphases are present in the narrative. On one hand, it stresses the anxiety of Jesus, which is ultimately resolved by a determination to meet the hour at hand. On the other hand, it also stresses the insensitivity of the disciples. Jesus, determined to do the will of God, moved through grief to make a decision for God. The disciples, blinded by their own interests, slept. Three times Jesus went deeper into the garden to pray alone, and three times he returned to find the disciples sleeping.

Jesus was struggling. He agonized over his decision. Prostrate on the ground before God, he asked for another way. Was this cup of suffering really necessary?

His prayers showed movement. While the first prayer sought the removal of the cup, the second prayer was resigned to the will of God that he must drink the cup of suffering. After the third prayer, Jesus fully embraced the mission. Instead of fleeing or hiding from the betrayer, he went out to meet him.

Prayer is regularly a struggle. We not only seek the will of God, but when we find it, it is often difficult to embrace it. We question, and we petition for alternatives. Jesus did as well. As disciples of Jesus, we, too, enter our own gardens of angst to agonize over obedience to the will of God. As disciples of Jesus, we, too, learn obedience through such experiences and possibly emerge from a garden of weeping to do the will of God.

QUESTION: As you remember a night in prayer, describe and reflect on the agony of that night.

PRAYER: *We want to do your will, O Lord; help our unbelief!*

THE MESSIAH IS CRUCIFIED

TEXT: LUKE 22:52–53

Then Jesus said to the chief priests, the officers of the temple police, and the elders who had come for him, "Have you come out with swords and clubs as if I were a bandit? When I was with you day after day in the temple, you did not lay hands on me. But this is your hour, and the power of darkness!"

Though there are several aspects of the movie that disturb me, one of the treasures I find in Mel Gibson's *The Passion of the Christ* is how darkness pervades the first third of the film. Gibson captures the mood, but he also captures the reign of darkness on that Friday.

The account of the crucifixion in the Gospel of Luke begins and ends with darkness. As the temple guards, elders, and chief priests arrested Jesus in the garden, Jesus announced, "this is your hour—when darkness reigns" (Luke 22:53 NIV). Darkness reigned till Jesus breathed his last, and Jesus died in darkness as God blocked out the Sun (Luke 22:44). Good Friday was a dark day, epitomizing the darkness that enveloped the world and symbolizing the darkness that has choked the world since humanity was exiled east of Eden. Good Friday was the hour of evil's seeming triumph. On that day, Satan's reign tyrannized the Son of God, Israel's Messiah.

The passion narrative provides amble evidence of that tyranny, which, unfortunately, is evident in our own world today.

When darkness reigns:

- Good people fail to pray.
- Friends betray friends.
- Swords are drawn.
- Disciples deny their teacher.
- The innocent are convicted.
- The guilty are released.
- The law is subverted for interests of power and control.
- The righteous are mocked.
- Women weep over the loss of their children.
- Soldiers demean and torture others.
- The condemned insult each other.
- The innocent are executed.

Luke's picture is shrouded in gloom from the garden to the cross, but his canvass also has rays of light, as a dawning Sun breaks into the darkness (Luke 1:78–79).

Even as darkness reigns, Jesus reveals the light of the kingdom. Even when darkness reigns, the kingdom of God cannot be smothered and snuffed out. Instead, beautiful and profound colors appear.

Though darkness reigns . . .

- Kingdom people refuse to use the sword even when threatened; Jesus said, "No more of this!" (Luke 22:51).
- Kingdom people pursue the will of God despite the consequences; Jesus said, "yet, not my will, but yours be done" (Luke 22:42).
- Kingdom people confidently anticipate with hope the fulfillment of kingdom; Jesus said, "the Son of Man will be seated at the right hand of the power of God" (Luke 22:69).
- Kingdom people weep for the brokenness of the world rather than over their own suffering for the sake of the kingdom; Jesus said, "do not weep for me; weep for yourselves and for your children" (Luke 23:28).

- Kingdom people forgive their persecutors; Jesus said, "Father, forgive them" (Luke 23:34).
- Kingdom people invite others into the kingdom; Jesus said, "Today you will be with me in paradise (Luke 23:43).
- Kingdom people trust in God's work despite the reign of darkness; Jesus said, "Father, into your hands I commit my spirit" (Luke 23:46 NIV).

Kingdom people follow Jesus. They, like Simon from Cyrene, pick up the cross and follow him. Kingdom people assault the powers of evil by submitting to the will of God and trusting in the promise of the coming kingdom.

Darkness reigned on Good Friday, but the kingdom of God also broke into that darkness. Even as darkness reigns in our day, we, as kingdom people, are called to follow Jesus—though doing so may take us to a cross.

QUESTION: In what ways does darkness surround you today, and where do you see the kingdom of God in the midst of the darkness?

PRAYER: *Darkness overwhelms us, O God; give us strength to be your light in the world.*

THE MESSIAH ON THE CROSS

TEXT: LUKE 23:32–47

Two others also, who were criminals, were led away to be put to death with him. When they came to the place that is called The Skull, they crucified Jesus there with the criminals, one on his right and one on his left. Then Jesus said, "Father, forgive them; for they do not know what they are doing." And they cast lots to divide his clothing. And the people stood by, watching; but the leaders scoffed at him, saying, "He saved others; let him save himself if he is the Messiah of God, his chosen one!" The soldiers also mocked him, coming up and offering him sour wine, and saying, "If you are the King of the Jews, save yourself!" There was also an inscription over him, "This is the King of the Jews."

One of the criminals who were hanged there kept deriding him and saying, "Are you not the Messiah? Save yourself and us!" But the other rebuked him, saying, "Do you not fear God, since you are under the same sentence of condemnation? And we indeed have been condemned justly, for we are getting what we deserve for our deeds, but this man has done nothing wrong." Then he said, "Jesus, remember me when you come into your kingdom." He replied, "Truly I tell you, today you will be with me in Paradise."

It was now about noon, and darkness came over the whole land until three in the afternoon, while the sun's light failed; and the curtain of the temple was torn in two. Then Jesus, crying with a loud voice, said, "Father, into your hands I commend my spirit." Having said this, he breathed his last. When the centurion saw what had taken place, he praised God and said, "Certainly this man was innocent."

The death of Jesus the Messiah is an enigma in so many ways. Something happened at the cross that changed the world, but exactly how and in what way is not absolutely clear. Whatever happened on the cross between God, Jesus, humanity, and the cosmos lies deep within the recesses of God's heart. Its mystery transcends our understanding, but we are not left clueless.

While there are many different ways to understand the cross, and Christian history has debated them for centuries, each Gospel tells the story of the Messiah's trial and death. Each has its own message and emphasis. Each expresses the mystery in a particular way, and Luke's Gospel is particularly poignant. Luke's passion narrative quotes Jesus three times, and each saying of the crucified Jesus points us to both the inscrutability and transformative nature of the cross.

Surrounded by people who falsely accused him, mocked him, beat him, divided his last possessions among themselves, and nailed him to the cross, Jesus prayed, "Father, forgive them; for they do not know what they are doing" (Luke 23:34). The cross and forgiveness are an unnatural pair, but, in part, the cross is designed for forgiveness. The blood of the new covenant forgives sins, and because of the cross—somehow and in some way—we receive God's forgiveness.

When one of the criminals crucified with the Messiah confessed his guilt, recognized the innocence of Jesus, and asked to be remembered when Jesus came into his kingdom, Jesus responded, "Truly I tell you, today you will be with me in Paradise." The sign over Jesus's head read, "the King of the Jews." The cross, as unlikely as it seems, was a kingdom moment. Indeed, it was the moment when Jesus absorbed all the evil that the powers—whether spiritual or political—threw at him. Jesus surrendered himself to the will of God through obedience for the sake of the kingdom of God. The cross was not the victory that evil powers imagined, but the beginning of their fall. Even on the cross, the kingdom of God testified to its sovereignty over evil. Evil would not win.

When darkness covered the whole land, Jesus, in a loud voice, cried out, "Father, into your hands I commend my spirit." The cross, we might think, is the last place we might entrust ourselves to God's purposes and trust that God is able to give meaning even to the most despicable evils committed by the powers. Though the cross had no seeming purpose, as an innocent and good person died there, its meaning was global, cosmic, and redemptive.

If we had been standing before the cross some two thousand years ago, there was nothing about that scene that announced the forgiveness of sin, victory over evil, and trust in God's good work. Crucifixion was a place of imperial vengeance, defeat through death, and mocking by one's enemies. Indeed, we probably would have wondered, as we often do today, where God was. Why did not God save this innocent one from death? Why did God abandon the Messiah?

Whatever our reasonings, the Messiah himself sought forgiveness for his persecutors, hoped in the victory his death entailed, and died with a profound trust in the God of Israel. What gives birth to such merciful love, expectant hope, and trusting faith? Jesus knew that though God abandoned him on the cross, God would not abandon him in the grave. The cross was not the final act in the theodrama; there was more to the story.

QUESTION: Though evil surrounded Jesus, how did he bear witness to the kingdom of God, and how do we imitate Jesus in our own lives?

PRAYER: *God, fill our hearts with forgiveness and trust in your good purposes even though we are surrounded by evil.*

THE MESSIAH IS ABANDONED

TEXT: MARK 15:33–37

When it was noon, darkness came over the whole land until three in the afternoon. At three o'clock Jesus cried out with a loud voice, "Eloi, Eloi, lema sabachthani?" which means, "My God, my God, why have you forsaken me?" When some of the bystanders heard it, they said, "Listen, he is calling for Elijah." And someone ran, filled a sponge with sour wine, put it on a stick, and gave it to him to drink, saying, "Wait, let us see whether Elijah will come to take him down." Then Jesus gave a loud cry and breathed his last.

Dying on that Friday afternoon, Jesus shouted, "My God, my God, why have you forsaken me?" (Mark 15:34). This expressed profound emotion. It gave witness to the depth of his human experience. It was an honest exclamation and an authentic question. But it did not so much accuse as it lamented, and this arose from the intimacy Jesus shared with his God.

Some hear the cry as a kind of relational abandonment in which God turned his back on Jesus because Jesus had become sin by bearing the sins of the world in that moment. Others hear the cry as an expression of some sort of tear or break in the fellowship of the triune God, in which God experienced alienation within God's own life—that is, the Father and the Son were alienated from each other.

Certainly, God mourned the death of the Son, and through the experience of the Son, the Father also suffered with the Son because of their transparent, shared intimacy. Also, the Spirit, who had rested upon the Son since his baptism, groaned with the Father and the Son in that moment. The pathos of suffering is not alien to God. Through the Son, God suffered, and God suffered as Father, Son, and Spirit. The cross was the mourning of God; it was divine as well as human lament.

But the unity of the Trinity was not ripped apart. Their communion did not waver. The Son trusted the Father, and, quoting Psalm 31:5, the Son entrusted himself to the Father (Luke 23:46). The Father did not abandon Jesus in death, and neither did the Son lose faith in the Father. The triune communion remained fully intact.

Rather than relational abandonment, the cross was the moment when the Son was embraced by the Father's love, and the Spirit continued to rest upon him. This is wonderfully depicted by Masaccio's fresco (1425–26) in the Santa Maria Novella church in Florence, Italy. The fresco is located high on a wall. As we lift our eyes, we first see Jesus hanging on the cross; then we see the Spirit, as a dove, hovering like a mother bird over the Son; and then, finally, we see the Father, facing the cross and extending loving arms toward the Son. We see the Trinity gathered—one on the cross, one resting on the head of crucified, and one lovingly towering in the background. The Father stands behind the cross with his arms outstretched as if embracing the Son as he hangs on the cross. Far from turning his back on the Son, the Father loves the Son, encircles the Son, and assures the Son of the Father's love. The Spirit, as a dove, rests upon the Son. Just as the dove descended on the Son at his baptism and anointed him with power, and just as the Spirit led the Son into the wilderness and throughout his ministry, so now in death the Spirit is still with the Son. The Trinity is united at the cross; there is no break in the triune communion.

At the same time, the Father abandoned the Son to death, though the Father did not abandon him on the cross. The Father abandoned the Son to death, but the Father did not abandon him in death. The Father abandoned the Son, just like the Father does us, to the grave, but God did not abandon the Son in the grave. By the power of the Spirit, who rested upon the Son, God raised the Son from the dead, and in the same way God, by the power of the Spirit, will raise us from the dead in the likeness of the Son.

The cross teaches us that while God abandons us to death, God will not abandon us in the grave. This is our hope, and it is our comfort.

QUESTION: Did God abandon Jesus?

PRAYER: *You are faithful, O God; though you abandoned your Son to the grave, you did not abandon him in the grave.*

THE MESSIAH IS VINDICATED

TEXT: MATTHEW 28:5–10

The angel said to the women, "Do not be afraid; I know that you are looking for Jesus who was crucified. He is not here; for he has been raised, as he said. Come, see the place where he lay. Then go quickly and tell his disciples, 'He has been raised from the dead, and indeed he is going ahead of you to Galilee; there you will see him.' This is my message for you." So they left the tomb quickly with fear and great joy, and ran to tell his disciples. Suddenly Jesus met them and said, "Greetings!" And they came to him, took hold of his feet, and worshiped him. Then Jesus said to them, "Do not be afraid; go and tell my brothers to go to Galilee; there they will see me."

The early preaching of the apostles in the Book of Acts has a consistent refrain. The Roman and Jewish authorities, the powers that ruled the world in Palestine, crucified Jesus, but God raised him from the dead. They condemned him, but God vindicated him. They rejected him, but God chose him as the chief cornerstone of God's new temple. In Jesus, God sided with the innocent, the oppressed, and the persecuted. God justified Jesus in the flesh through his resurrection.

According to the apostle Paul, Jesus was delivered over to death for our offenses and was raised for "our justification" (Rom. 4:25) so that we might be saved by "his life" (Rom. 5:10). But first it was the justification of Jesus himself. When God raised Jesus from the dead, the judgment of death (curse) was reversed, and the just one was vindicated. This is the "mystery" of godliness (1 Tim. 3:16 NIV). Death did not win. The resurrection of Jesus destroyed death, and his resurrection became our resurrection. When Jesus was raised from the dead, it was a pledge of our own resurrection. We were, in effect, raised with Jesus.

Our resurrection with Jesus is the presence of God's transforming Spirit. The life we now live is not our own—it is the resurrected life of Jesus (Rom. 6:11; Gal. 2:20). We live in the power of the life-giving Spirit who has given us new life in Christ. The presence of the Spirit is God's gift by which God transforms us into the image of Christ. Thus, the present experience of the transforming power of the Spirit bears fruit in us and is a foretaste of our full redemption by the power of the Spirit in the future resurrection (Rom. 8:11–12).

Our resurrection with Jesus also transforms our experience of death. Since God has defeated death, we no longer fear its hostile grip. Consequently, our experience of death is transformed from hopelessness, fear, and despair into hope, expectation, and anticipation. Though we no longer fear death, we hate it as it defaces God's good creation.

Our resurrection with Jesus in our "spiritual" bodies enables full communion with God in the new heaven and new Earth. Since God has raised Christ with a "spiritual body" (1 Cor. 15:44), we yearn for our spiritual bodies when we will experience the fullness of God's Spirit in the new heaven and new Earth. Indeed, the indwelling Spirit is our promise that we will be raised, and the power of the Spirit that now works in us to transform us into divine glory will transform our broken bodies into the glorious body of Jesus Christ (Rom. 8:11; Phil. 3:21). Our present mortal, weak, and broken bodies will be transformed into immortal, powerful, and glorious bodies. We will have bodies energized and empowered by the full transforming presence of the Spirit of God (1 Cor. 15:42–49).

The resurrection is God's pledge to perfect the world in new creation. God acted decisively to reverse the effects of Good Friday. The resurrection is God's pledge to birth a new heaven and a new Earth and to liberate the cosmos from its bondage. The resurrection is new creation.

QUESTION: What is the significance of the resurrection of Jesus?

PRAYER: *We praise you, O God, because you have not abandoned us in death.*

AT THE TABLE WITH THE MESSIAH ON RESURRECTION SUNDAY

TEXT: LUKE 24:30–35

When he was at the table with them, he took bread, blessed and broke it, and gave it to them. Then their eyes were opened, and they recognized him; and he vanished from their sight. They said to each other, "Were not our hearts burning within us while he was talking to us on the road, while he was opening the scriptures to us?" That same hour they got up and returned to Jerusalem; and they found the eleven and their companions gathered together. They were saying, "The Lord has risen indeed, and he has appeared to Simon!" Then they told what had happened on the road, and how he had been made known to them in the breaking of the bread.

On Resurrection Day, nearly two thousand years ago, two disciples, according to Luke 24, were transformed by their experience of the risen Messiah at a table in Emmaus.

While walking to Emmaus, they heard the story of a Messiah who must first suffer and then enter glory. The stranger who walked with them expounded Scripture, and their hearts burned within them as they saw the story of God in new ways. As the Scriptures were opened, so were their hearts.

At a table in the city of Emmaus, the stranger took the bread, blessed God, broke it, and gave it to the two disciples. In that moment, the risen Messiah was "made known" to these disciples in the breaking of the bread.

What happened in the breaking of the bread? What continues to happen in the breaking of the bread? At the table, the living Messiah is "made known" within the community of disciples. When disciples of Jesus are gathered around the table, Jesus is present and, more importantly, Jesus is revealed.

Jesus said as much earlier in Luke: "This is my body" and "This cup . . . is the new covenant in my blood" (Luke 22:19–20).

The problem is the meaning of *is*, which depends on what the meaning of *is* is, right?

Paul expands the *is* in 1 Corinthians 10:16: "Is" not the breaking of bread "a sharing in the blood of Christ," and "is" not the cup "a sharing in the body of Christ"? When we eat the bread and drink the cup, we participate or share in the blessing, and we commune with the one who gave himself for us. We share in the benefits of God's work in Christ, and we experience what the body and blood of Jesus procure for us. We experience peace with God, and we are assured of God's grace, which God provides at the table.

Luke provides his own explanation in Luke 24:35. At the table, the living Jesus is "made known" or revealed. The relationship between the sign (bread and wine) and the thing signified (body and blood) is not merely symbolic or representative, but neither is the nature or substance of the sign changed.

The bread and wine become a means by which the living Christ is revealed. It is an epiphany, which reveals and visibly communicates the reality of the living Christ in the community. The table becomes more than a cognitive remembrance in which we learn something about Christ. The table becomes a means by which we experience the living Christ and participate in the reality of the new creation, inaugurated by the resurrection of Jesus.

At the table, Jesus reveals the future, we remember the future, and we experience the future. The table is an epiphany—we see the future! Death will not win; Christ has already won!

Every Resurrection Day, disciples all over the world gather around a table where the living Christ is "made known." We not only learn about Christ; we experience Christ. We not only learn about the new creation inaugurated by the resurrection of Jesus; we taste it.

Blessed be the name of the Lord, who did not leave us in the dust of death but has given us new life through Jesus, who is our life.

QUESTION: In what ways do you experience the living Christ at the table of the Lord?

PRAYER: *Make known to us, O Lord, your Messiah in the breaking of the bread.*

THE MESSIAH COMMISSIONS HIS DISCIPLES

TEXT: MATTHEW 28:18–20

And Jesus came and said to them, "All authority in heaven and on earth has been given to me. Go therefore and make disciples of all nations, baptizing them in the name of the Father and of the Son and of the Holy Spirit, and teaching them to obey everything that I have commanded you. And remember, I am with you always, to the end of the age."

Between his resurrection and his ascension to the right hand of God, Jesus spent forty days with his disciples teaching them about the kingdom of God and his messianic role. He opened their minds to understand the Scriptures and to understand everything that was written about the Messiah in the Torah, the prophetic books, and the psalms.

In essence, Jesus gave them a message to share. They were to proclaim the name of Jesus to all the nations. This involved announcing the good news of the kingdom of God, the death and resurrection of Jesus, the forgiveness of sins, and the end of Israel's exile, as well as the inclusion of the nations in the kingdom of God. The disciples, however, would not do this alone, but in the power of the Holy Spirit.

Jesus prepared them for their anointing in the Spirit when God would pour out the Spirit upon them (Acts 1). They were told to wait in Jerusalem for the promise of the Father, which was their baptism in the Spirit. Just as Jesus was anointed with power in the Spirit at his baptism, the restoration of the kingdom to Israel would begin when God anointed these disciples with power in the Spirit. This anointing would empower them to become witnesses to the work of God in Jesus and testify to the reality of the kingdom of God, beginning in Jerusalem and extending to the ends of the known world.

God, according to Isaiah 49:6, commissioned Israel to be a light to nations and to extend the salvation of God to the ends of the Earth. This was also the mission of Israel's Messiah. As disciples of Jesus, it is also our mission (Acts 13:47). As God pours out the Spirit upon the disciples, God empowers them to continue the mission of Israel, which is to bring salvation to the ends of the Earth.

The Gospel of Matthew records this commission in its last few verses. Though the ministry of Jesus was primarily to Israel, when Jesus gathered his disciples for some final words, he commissioned them to "make disciples of all nations." Jesus told his disciples to take his message to all nations and to disciple the nations, just as he had discipled them. The mission of Jesus is not stationary or passive. Instead, it moves throughout the world and proactively invites others to follow and become part of the community of Jesus.

From the beginning, God intended to fill the Earth with God's glory as human beings, the imagers of God, flourished. God chose Israel to renew that glory not only in their own land but to the ends of the Earth. God sent the Messiah to give abundant life, and the Messiah sent his disciples among the nations to proclaim that life.

Just as Israel was baptized in the sea and under the clouds in their exodus from Egyptian slavery, and just as the Messiah was anointed with the Spirit at his baptism, so Jesus commissions the disciples to baptize those who seek to follow Jesus and teach them how to live as his disciples. When they are baptized, they are included in the community or the fellowship of the Father, Son, and Spirit. They become part of the kingdom of God; they become part of Israel's story.

As part of Israel's story, they are called to embody and practice the ethics of the kingdom of God. Because they are included in the communion of the Father, Son, and Holy Spirit, they are called to imitate God and invite others into that community by making disciples of all nations.

QUESTION: What is the significance of the Great Commission of Jesus the Messiah?

PRAYER: *Empower us, O God, to participate in your mission for the sake of the nations.*

THE MESSIAH IS ENTHRONED AS LORD

TEXT: EPHESIANS 1:20–23

God put this power to work in Christ when he raised him from the dead and seated him at his right hand in the heavenly places, far above all rule and authority and power and dominion, and above every name that is named, not only in this age but also in the age to come. And he has put all things under his feet and has made him the head over all things for the church, which is his body, the fullness of him who fills all in all.

Jesus, resurrected from the dead and exalted to the right hand of the Father, is the fountainhead of new humanity. He is new humanity and thus the ground of new creation.

Jesus was not simply resuscitated from the dead, but he was transformed from a dying human to a glorious, resurrected one. Born in the present age and thus bound over to death, he was raised from the dead to live in a new creation. His resurrection was the beginning of the triumphant renewal of creation. His resurrection body was new creation.

The body of Jesus, just like our bodies, was deeply entangled with the creation. Our bodies are from the dust of the Earth. We, as flesh and bones, are part of the creation. We are the material imagers of God within the material creation. But within the present age—this "present evil age," as Paul called it (Gal. 1:4)—our bodies are degenerating, declining, and dying.

The resurrection of Jesus, however, was the reversal of this decay. It was new creation through the transformation of that broken, dying body into a glorious body. It was not the creation of something new, however. Rather, it was the renewal of something old. Through the resurrection, God by the power of the Spirit made the body of Jesus new. It was regenerated, renewed, and transformed—never to die again.

The resurrection of Jesus injected a regenerating power into the cosmos. The newness and glory of the resurrected body of Jesus was the beginning of the newness and glory of the new creation, which will remake, renew, and transform the cosmos itself. Jesus was "firstborn from the dead" (Col. 1:18), not only in the sense that he was the first, but he is "firstborn" because he has the preeminence as the one who sustains, grounds, and empowers the new creation itself.

Just as resurrection was new creation, so also the exaltation of Jesus to the right hand of the Creator is the reign of Christ over the old creation until all things become new. Jesus will reign until the last enemy—which is death—is destroyed, and the death Jesus will destroy is that power of death that reigns not only over humanity but over the creation itself.

The exaltation of Jesus is the assured Word of God that death will be defeated, the creation will be redeemed, and humanity will be fully restored to its co-regency with God in the cosmos. Humanity will sit on the throne with Jesus to reign over the new creation, and humanity, along with Jesus, will share in the materiality of that new creation with resurrected bodies.

Eden—with all the symbolism attached to that name—will be renewed, but more than that, Eden will be glorified as new creation, just as the body of Jesus was glorified.

The resurrection and exaltation of Jesus are the "already" of our "not yet" future. God has accomplished redemption in Jesus. The act of God in Jesus, the resurrection of Jesus within history, is the assurance of the future. And the Spirit of God bears witness to this assurance because the gift of the Holy Spirit in our hearts is the guarantee of that future. Jesus is king and sits on the throne of David as Israel's Messiah.

QUESTION: What is the meaning of the exaltation of Jesus as Lord, and why is this an important moment in the life of Jesus?

PRAYER: *God, we confess that you have made Jesus both Lord and Messiah, and you have enthroned him at your right hand as king.*

NEW CREATION INAUGURATED

TEXT: GALATIANS 6:14–16

May I never boast of anything except the cross of our Lord Jesus Christ, by which the world has been crucified to me, and I to the world. For neither circumcision nor uncircumcision is anything; but a new creation is everything! As for those who will follow this rule—peace be upon them, and mercy, and upon the Israel of God.

Creation is good, but new creation is better. The present creation, though it retains its inherent goodness, is presently frustrated because it is bound over to corruption. It awaits something better; it awaits a glorious liberation. The present bondage will pass away even as the creation itself is gloriously transfigured when the new heaven and new Earth appear.

As the present form of the world is even now passing away, the new creation is already present. The children of God experience the first fruits of the new creation through the presence of the Spirit who transforms them from glory to glory (2 Cor. 3:18). By this, the children of God are new creatures renewed in the image of their Creator. Yet, the children of God, along with the creation itself, groan for full adoption through the redemption of their bodies. This new humanity, already present by the Spirit through the renewal of our inner persons, will fully appear in the resurrection.

New humanity is grounded in the new human, Jesus the Messiah. The glorified Lord is new creation. He reversed the brokenness under which creation groans as the kingdom entered the world through his ministry in the power of the Spirit. He transformed death as the firstborn from the dead by the will of God. His Adamic body was transformed into a new body, animated by the Spirit of God through which the ascended Messiah reigns in heaven. At the right hand of God, ever interceding for the people of God, he has poured out the Spirit upon the church in order to transform them into a new community, a new creation. Jesus, as the glorified new human, will return to redeem humanity and inaugurate the new heaven and new Earth so the glory of God may fill the creation.

This new humanity, embodied in the resurrected and exalted Jesus, is the ground of new creation. That new life is our life. Jesus's new creation kingdom ministry is our ministry. The second Adam's life-giving body is our future body. Just as the old Adamic life passed away in the ministry, death, and resurrection of Jesus, so our lives—inwardly renewed and outwardly redeemed—participate in the new life revealed in the new humanity of the ascended Lord. Just as our old Adamic life is transformed into a new and glorious freedom, so the creation itself will share in the joy of the children of God.

This story—the movement from the old age to the new age—is pregnant with meaning. As new creatures, we live by the ethic of the new creation. As people translated into the kingdom of God, we live as if the kingdom of God has already come, and in some sense, it already has. We embrace the vision, ethic, and mission of the new creation embodied in the incarnation, ministry, death, resurrection, and ascension of Jesus the Messiah.

For these reasons, and more, in Galatians 6:16 Paul identifies not only the cross but new creation as the rule or canon by which Christians walk. The richness, depth, and visionary importance of this theme defines Christianity. It points us to the future when God will fully realize the goal for which God created us.

QUESTION: In what ways do you experience new creation in your life?

PRAYER: *Increase our faith, O Lord, that we might more deeply and fully experience your new creation.*

ACT FOUR

CHURCH

THE RENEWAL OF ISRAEL

TEXT: ACTS 1:6–8

So when they had come together, they asked him, "Lord, is this the time when you will restore the kingdom to Israel?" He replied, "It is not for you to know the times or periods that the Father has set by his own authority. But you will receive power when the Holy Spirit has come upon you; and you will be my witnesses in Jerusalem, in all Judea and Samaria, and to the ends of the earth."

Only seven weeks ago, the future looked bleak. The one whom they thought was the Messiah was dead. The disciples of Jesus hid in fear, and their spirits were broken. They had lost all hope.

But that changed when God raised Jesus from the dead, and Jesus appeared to his disciples on different occasions over a period of forty days. When he appeared, he ate with them, studied the Hebrew Scriptures with them, and taught them about the good news of the kingdom of God.

At the end of the forty days, Jesus told them to remain in Jerusalem and wait for the promise of the Father, who was the Holy Spirit. The disciples, who had listened to Jesus teach about the kingdom of God over those past forty days, recognized that the coming of the Spirit was also the coming of the kingdom of God. They knew God had promised to restore the kingdom to Israel, and the promise of the Spirit meant that God was about to inaugurate it.

Jesus did not say their expectation was wrong or misguided. Instead, they should not concern themselves about the timing of the kingdom's coming. Jesus told them to wait, and God would send the Spirit in God's own good time.

Then Jesus left. He ascended to the right hand of God. While we tend to think of this in spatial terms, the primary point is royal. Jesus, Israel's Messiah, was escorted into the presence of the Ancient of Days by the angelic hosts and was given authority, glory, and a kingdom (Dan. 7:13–14). Jesus was enthroned at the right hand of God and now ruled over a kingdom that would never end. He will reign until all the principalities and powers upon the Earth are defeated, and the last enemy he will defeat is death itself.

But the disciples must wait. The disciples, one hundred and twenty of them (including Mary, the mother of Jesus and other women), waited in Jerusalem for the restoration of the kingdom to Israel through the gift of the Holy Spirit. They waited for the promised descent of the Spirit from the one who ascended to the throne.

God waited until the last day of the feast of Pentecost. God restored the kingdom to Israel on Pentecost. This harvest festival celebrated God's gracious provision. Pentecost began seven weeks earlier but was celebrated in a climactic way on the fiftieth day of the festival, which was the eighth first day of the week since Passover. In Acts 2, Pentecost happened on the last day of the Festival, the first day of the eighth week.

On Pentecost, God, through the enthroned Messiah, poured out the Spirit upon the disciples. They reaped the harvest of the resurrection and enthronement of the Messiah. Though Roman power, with the consent of Jewish authorities and a mob at Passover, killed the Messiah, God raised him from the dead and seated him at God's own right hand. In this way, God restored the kingdom to Israel through the reign of Jesus, whom God declared both "Lord and Messiah" (Acts 2:36). God restored the Davidic dynasty. A son of David ruled in Israel once again. And the harvest of this new reign of God was the pouring out of the Holy Spirit, and this is where the story of a new creation community begins.

QUESTION: In what ways did Jesus prepare his disciples for their future witness?

PRAYER: *Equip us, O God, for your mission.*

THE POURING OUT OF THE SPIRIT

TEXT: ACTS 2:16–21

This is what was spoken through the prophet Joel:
"In the last days it will be, God declares,
that I will pour out my Spirit upon all flesh,
and your sons and your daughters shall prophesy,
and your young men shall see visions,
and your old men shall dream dreams.
Even upon my slaves, both men and women,
in those days I will pour out my Spirit;
and they shall prophesy.
And I will show portents in the heaven above
and signs on the earth below,
blood, and fire, and smoky mist.
The sun shall be turned to darkness
and the moon to blood,
before the coming of the Lord's great and glorious day.
Then everyone who calls on the name of the Lord shall be saved."

One hundred and twenty disciples, men and women, were gathered in a room waiting for the promised Holy Spirit, who would empower them to bear witness to the reign of God's Messiah to the ends of the Earth. Finally, their waiting came to end. God poured out the Spirit upon them, and they were each filled with the Spirit. It was Pentecost, the fiftieth day after Passover. It was the first day of the week.

The significance of this moment is difficult to overestimate. Whatever we say about it is less than what it fully means. It was a surprising work of God that exploded all expectations, anticipations, and limitations. On the day of Pentecost, Peter announced that this descent of the Spirit from the heavens was what the prophet Joel had foretold centuries earlier.

What Joel envisioned was the veritable shaking of the cosmos to its core. It was as if the universe had reversed its course. The light of the Sun was darkened, and the light of the Moon became blood red. Heaven and Earth were on fire!

What ignited the cosmos? At Pentecost, God poured out the Holy Spirit upon Israel! With this, God shattered the limitations of the old creation, with all its brokenness and divisions, and poured into it the dynamics of the new creation that flow from the reign of Messiah at the right hand of God. The world had changed.

Throughout its history with God, Israel knew the empowering presence of the Spirit. In the wilderness, God took "some of the spirit that was on [Moses] and put it on the seventy elders; and when the spirit rested upon them, they prophesied" (Num. 11:25). At that time, Moses prayed that God would put the Spirit upon all the Lord's people.

Now that day had come. We call it Pentecost. God poured out the Spirit upon all Israel, but not only Israel. "All flesh" would receive the Spirit of God, which is the inclusion of Gentiles, the inclusion of all ethnicities or races, among God's people. Moreover, not only elders in Israel but the youth of Jews and Gentiles would see visions. Even more, it would not only be the recently liberated elders of Israel, but enslaved Jews and Gentiles would also prophesy. And further, it would not only be men who would prophesy and dream dreams, but women would also be empowered by God to see visions and prophesy.

We might think about it this way. Before Pentecost, typically though not exclusively, free Jewish males led the people of God. But Pentecost changed this. The pouring of the Spirit in Acts 2, in fulfillment of Joel's prophecy, enlarged the community of gifted leadership from free Jewish men to enslaved Gentile women.

The gifts that the ascended Messiah gave to the Lord's people were not restricted to Jews but included all races, they were not restricted to free peoples but included the enslaved, and they were not restricted to men but included women.

Pentecost shifted the dynamics. Those once excluded were now included, and those once unchosen were now chosen. All races, the enslaved, and women were now empowered and gifted for participation in the mission of God.

QUESTION: How is Pentecost revolutionary and earthshaking?

PRAYER: *May your Spirit, O God, open our eyes to see how you have broken down the walls of separation and discrimination.*

THE INVITATION INTO COMMUNITY

Baptism

TEXT: ACTS 2:37–41

Now when they heard this, they were cut to the heart and said to Peter and to the other apostles, "Brothers, what should we do?" Peter said to them, "Repent, and be baptized every one of you in the name of Jesus Christ so that your sins may be forgiven; and you will receive the gift of the Holy Spirit. For the promise is for you, for your children, and for all who are far away, everyone whom the Lord our God calls to him." And he testified with many other arguments and exhorted them, saying, "Save yourselves from this corrupt generation." So those who welcomed his message were baptized, and that day about three thousand persons were added.

Filled with the Spirit, Peter, on the day of Pentecost, proclaimed the good news of the kingdom of God.

Jesus was a prophet attested by God through many signs, but the ruling powers crucified him. Though unjust hands killed Jesus, God raised him from the dead. Peter himself, along with others, testified to the reality of this resurrection. Raised, Jesus was exalted to the right hand of God as Lord and Messiah, and it was from this exalted position that Jesus poured out the Spirit upon these witnesses. The good news is that the Messiah reigns.

But this was disturbing news to those who were convicted of their participation in the rejection of God's anointed. What were they to do? How might they find forgiveness and become participants in the reign of the Messiah?

The brief answer, according to Acts 2, is something like this: commit to Jesus, repent of your sins, pass through the waters with Jesus, and share in the communal journey through the wilderness into the new heaven and new Earth. In this way, God forgives sins and gifts the people with the Spirit. On the day of Pentecost, three thousand people were added to the community of the one hundred and twenty through repentance and baptism, and that community devoted themselves to life together, including listening to the apostles' teaching, fellowship, breaking of bread, and prayers.

Faced with the horror that they had killed the Messiah and recognizing the fulfillment of Joel 2, some were "cut to the heart" (Acts 2:37) and wanted to know what to do. Peter's response in Acts 2:38–39 sounds familiar (John the Baptizer had a similar message) but was new: "Repent, and be baptized every one of you in the name of Jesus Christ so that your sins may be forgiven; and you will receive the gift of the Holy Spirit. For the promise is for you, for your children, and for all who are far away."

Peter's invitation reminds us of the baptism of John, which was a baptism of repentance for the forgiveness of sins. But Peter's invitation also promised what belonged to the baptism of Jesus himself. When Jesus shared the waters of baptism with Israel, he was immersed in solidarity with his people. Coming up out of the water, however, he was anointed with the Holy Spirit, and this is what Peter promised Israel. Just as the Messiah joined Israel in the water, when Israel is baptized in the name of Jesus, they, too, are anointed with the Holy Spirit. Moreover, whoever is baptized in the name of Jesus is included in the promise, which is for them, their children, and to those who are far off. This is the Abrahamic promise that envisions the inclusion of the Gentiles through the blessing of the nations.

Allegiance to Jesus, repentance of sin, and baptism into Jesus the Messiah ushers all, Jew and Gentile, into the kingdom of God. We are baptized into the community of the Messiah, the body of Christ. As a people who belong to the Messiah, we are also heirs of the promise made to Abraham. We are heirs of the new heaven and the new Earth.

Baptism, by which we enter into the community of Jesus, is a means of forgiveness, a marker of inclusion, and a sign of the future. It is also a commitment to the mission of God as disciples of Jesus. We are now members of a Jesus community, committed to both the ethics of Jesus and his mission.

QUESTION: Do you remember your baptism? What was it like, and why were you baptized?

PRAYER: *We welcome, by your grace, O God, all who receive your word and are baptized in the name of Jesus.*

THE FORMATION OF COMMUNITY

Assembly

TEXT: ACTS 2:46–47

Day by day, as they spent much time together in the temple, they broke bread at home and ate their food with glad and generous hearts, praising God and having the goodwill of all the people. And day by day the Lord added to their number those who were being saved.

On the day of Pentecost, three thousand people were baptized into a new community. They embraced the good news of Jesus the Messiah, whom God had raised from the dead and exalted to the throne of David. In its early days, thousands were added to this community, including priests and Pharisees.

The restoration of Israel had begun. People joined Jesus in the water, and they, in effect, crossed the sea with ancient Israel through their baptism. Moreover, just as ancient Israel traveled to Mount Sinai and there encountered God's presence who came to dwell in Israel's tabernacle, so those who entered the water with Jesus encountered God's presence through the Holy Spirit who was poured out upon them.

Just as Israel was baptized in the sea and under the cloud, so renewed Israel was baptized in water. Just as Israel encountered God at Mount Sinai when they assembled before God's presence, so renewed Israel assembled in the presence of God as well. The same Israel that assembled at Mount Sinai in the first chapters of the Book of Acts assembled on Mount Zion. Israel referred to their first encounter with God as a gathered people at Mount Sinai as the "day of the assembly" (Deut. 9:10). On the day of Pentecost, renewed Israel gathered as the people of new creation. They assembled on the Lord's day.

The second chapter of Acts records that renewed Israel gathered daily both at the temple and in homes. These early believers met at the temple every day. There they listened to the apostles' teaching and prayed their prayers. Peter and John, for example, continued the daily habit of prayer in the temple every afternoon at three o'clock (Acts 3:1). And they, along with other apostles, taught the people daily in the temple (Acts 5:32).

This newly baptized people also met daily in their homes in order to break bread. They shared meals together, and they received this food with generous and grateful hearts filled with joy as they praised God for what God had done in Jesus.

We can imagine a daily assembly of thousands in the temple as they worshiped together, prayed together, and listened to the apostles' teaching, and we can imagine in the evening small groups of people meeting in homes to break bread.

Assembly is an important marker of the people of God. It was important for Israel who assembled weekly, monthly, and quarterly (approximately) for festive gatherings where they ate the sacrifices that were offered on the altar. They gathered for worship in the temple courts and at sacrificial meals.

Renewed Israel continued the practices of ancient Israel. Having passed through the water, they received the outpouring of the Holy Spirit, who came to dwell among the people of God. In response, renewed Israel gathered daily in the temple and in their homes to give thanks for their salvation, encourage one another, and dwell in God's presence together.

This is the reason renewed Israel, as it appears in the Book of Acts, is called the church or the *ecclesia*. The people are called the church because they are an assembly—a gathered people—in the presence of God and among whom God dwells. This is the meaning of the word *church*.

The people of God assemble. They are the church. They are God's gathered ones.

QUESTION: Why is assembly important for Christian formation, and how does the assembly form people as disciples of Jesus?

PRAYER: *"Gather to me, my faithful ones" (Ps. 50:5) you once said, O God, and we thank you that you invite us into your presence to enjoy you and seek your face.*

THE FORMATION OF COMMUNITY

The Teaching of the Apostles

TEXT: ACTS 2:42, 5:42

They devoted themselves to the apostles' teaching and fellowship, to the breaking of bread and the prayers. . . . And every day in the temple and at home they did not cease to teach and proclaim Jesus as the Messiah.

As renewed Israel gathered daily in the temple, they listened to the teaching of the apostles, and they committed themselves to that teaching.

The apostles were mentored by Jesus for three years during his earthly ministry. Also, during forty days after his resurrection, Jesus taught the apostles about the good news of the kingdom of God. Jesus had been preaching this gospel from the beginning, according to Luke 4, and he brought it home to the apostles during his post-resurrection gatherings with them. Further, in light of the pouring out of the Spirit in fulfillment of Joel 2, they understood the meaning and significance of God's reign through Jesus. Now, they were leaders of God's renewed community.

Since this newly gathered community of God listened to the apostles' teaching and devoted themselves to it, it is important to pause for a moment to listen to this teaching ourselves. This teaching shaped how the church lived out its life under the reign of God's Messiah.

From the beginning of the Book of Acts until its end, the primary topic of the preaching of the apostles—whether Peter or Paul—is the good news of the kingdom of God and the name of the Lord Jesus, the Messiah. This is what Jesus taught the apostles during their forty days with him at the beginning of the Book of Acts (Acts 1:3), and it is what Paul taught in Rome at the end of the Book of Acts (Acts 28:31).

But what does it mean to proclaim Jesus and the reign of God? When we read the sermons in Acts, we see a consistent emphasis on the theodrama.

God, the Creator of heaven and Earth, chose Israel as the firstborn among the nations to bless all other nations. Though Israel faltered in its faithfulness, God sent the Messiah, who is Jesus, into the world to lead Israel out of exile and invite all races into the kingdom of God to share in the Abrahamic promise. Jesus proved himself a prophet by the signs and wonders he performed and the good that he did. He called Israel back to a renewed life with God through repentance and embodied the good news of the reign of God in his own life and ministry. Though the ruling powers executed him, God raised him from the dead and vindicated his message and ministry. In this way, God inaugurated a new day for Israel and for the rest of humanity. God now reigns, and God, through the good news of the kingdom, calls people into a new life of faith, hope, and love.

The apostles, if their sermons in Acts are any indication, announced the theodrama. They told the story of God as it unfolded in Israel and came to its fulfillment in Jesus the Messiah. It is a story about God's mercy and faithfulness, a story about the Messiah who embodied authentic life, and a story about hope in the midst of brokenness.

The apostles taught about the kingdom of God and how Jesus reigns at the right hand of God. Like Jesus, they proclaimed the good news of the kingdom, and that good news—just as Jesus preached it—included the forgiveness of sins, the gift of the Holy Spirit, the liberation of the oppressed, and a future resurrection.

QUESTION: What did the apostles teach and emphasize in the Book of Acts?

PRAYER: *God, we commit to listening to and obeying the teaching of your apostles.*

THE FORMATION OF COMMUNITY

The Table of the Lord

TEXT: ACTS 20:7–12

On the first day of the week, when we met to break bread, Paul was holding a discussion with them; since he intended to leave the next day, he continued speaking until midnight. There were many lamps in the room upstairs where we were meeting. A young man named Eutychus, who was sitting in the window, began to sink off into a deep sleep while Paul talked still longer. Overcome by sleep, he fell to the ground three floors below and was picked up dead. But Paul went down, and bending over him took him in his arms, and said, "Do not be alarmed, for his life is in him." Then Paul went upstairs, and after he had broken bread and eaten, he continued to converse with them until dawn; then he left. Meanwhile they had taken the boy away alive and were not a little comforted.

As the newly formed community of Jesus followers assembled daily in the temple, they prayed together and listened to the teaching of the apostles. Small groups also gathered in homes to break bread together.

When Luke, the author of Acts, says that the disciples of Jesus were devoted to the breaking of bread and that they broke bread daily in their homes (Acts 2:42, 46), what does he mean by that language?

This is why it is important to read Luke's first volume, the Gospel of Luke. In his first volume, Luke describes how Jesus broke bread with five thousand as he fed the hungry who were following him (Luke 9:16), broke bread with his disciples during the Passover (Luke 22:19), and broke bread with two disciples at Emmaus on the day of his resurrection (Luke 24:30). In each case, the living Jesus acted as the Messiah of Israel by providing nourishment, both physical and spiritual. Jesus was the living host of these tables, both before and after his death. Particularly, in Luke 24, Jesus took the bread, gave thanks, broke it, and gave it to the two disciples in Emmaus. In that moment, Jesus was revealed to the disciples as the resurrected Messiah, once dead but now eternally alive. Jesus was made known to the disciples in the breaking of the bread (Luke 24:35).

When we read that the disciples in Acts 2 continued to break bread, we may take our cue from what Luke has already told us. Jesus, as the living, resurrected Messiah, continued to host a meal for his community. The disciples gathered daily in their homes to eat a meal together in which they gave thanks for what God had done in Jesus. In the breaking of bread, Jesus was revealed as the living Messiah. Consequently, disciples shared their food with joy and generosity.

In the early days of the Jesus community in Jerusalem, the disciples broke bread daily, and as the community spread across the Mediterranean basin, we learn that the disciples in Troas apparently gathered weekly in order to break bread. On the day of Pentecost, they broke bread on the first day of the week (Acts 20:7).

The confluence of breaking bread, the resurrection of a dead person, and the first day of the week in both Luke 24 and Acts 20 bears strong witness to a weekly gathering to sit at the table of the Lord, where the resurrected Messiah hosts the meal as a weekly celebration of his resurrection.

The table of the Lord, or the breaking of bread, is a meeting place. It is where individual believers encounter the risen Christ in community with other believers.

At that table, we hear a word of grace: "This is my body, which is given for you" (Luke 22:19), or, "this is my blood of the covenant, which is poured out for many for the forgiveness of sins" (Matt. 26:28). At that table, we hear a word of thanksgiving: We give thanks to God for the gift of the Messiah through the Spirit. At that table, we hear a communal word: We eat the same bread and drink the same cup as the one body of Christ.

The table, the breaking of bread, is a word of grace, thanksgiving, and community. It is where renewed Israel, as a gathered people, experiences the mercy of God and the joy of the Holy Spirit in the presence of the living Messiah as we hear the invitation of Jesus: Come to the table!

QUESTION: In what ways do you experience comfort and joy at the table of the Lord?

PRAYER: *At your table, O Lord, we celebrate your resurrection!*

THE FORMATION OF COMMUNITY

Fellowship

TEXT: ACTS 2:42, 44–45

They devoted themselves to the apostles' teaching and fellowship, to the breaking of bread and the prayers. . . . All who believed were together and had all things in common; they would sell their possessions and goods and distribute the proceeds to all, as any had need.

Formed on the day of Pentecost in Acts 2, this new community of Jesus followers "devoted themselves to the apostles' teaching and fellowship, to the breaking of bread and the prayers" (Acts 2:42). While it is possible to understand the breaking of bread and prayers as categories under the heading of "fellowship," the word *fellowship* also encompasses more than the breaking of bread and the prayers.

The word *fellowship*, though it includes those bonds that hold a community together, also refers to the material and physical dimensions of shared life together. They broke bread together, they prayed together, and they also shared their possessions with each other. Fellowship includes concrete acts of shared life.

Luke says this early community devoted itself to fellowship and then tells us that "all who believed were together and had all things in common" (Acts 2:44). The words *fellowship* and *common* are from the same Greek root. This community shared their resources with each other, as needed. It does not mean they held their property without any distinction, but their fellowship was such that they let go of their property in order to meet the needs of fellow believers. In this sense, "no one claimed private ownership of any possessions, but everything they owned was held in common" (Acts 4:32).

They sold their possessions in order to distribute to the needy in their community. Just as Jesus taught his disciples, they sold their possessions and gave to the poor (Luke 12:33, 14:33) so that no one among them had any material need. In this way, renewed Israel also remained faithful to the Torah, which taught that there should be no needy among the people. This included the needs of aliens and immigrants to the land, and Israel shared with them as well as their own families and nation. The goal to meet all needs in the land not only included their own kin, but also aliens who lived in the land with them (Deut. 26:12).

While fellowship is often conceived in terms of spiritual bonds and relationships—and those are parts of its meaning—the disciples in the early church were committed to sharing their material goods and possessions with each other so that no one went hungry or went without basic human needs.

In other words, fellowship in the early church was material, physical, and concrete. It was no mere handshake and "see you later" as we each retreat to our homes. It involved a shared life together, including shared possessions, shared meals, and shared prayers. It was authentic community with deep compassion for each other's material needs. And, as disciples of Jesus, they were willing to sell their possessions—to divest themselves of their own security and comfort—in order to provide for those who needed what they had.

The fellowship of the early church was tangible and compassionate. This shared life—in which people were willing to sell what they had so others might have what they need—characterized their communal life. As a result, people were attracted to them, and their community grew.

QUESTION: In what ways have you experienced this kind of fellowship among disciples of Jesus?

PRAYER: *What we have received from you, O God, we commit to share with others.*

THE FORMATION OF COMMUNITY

Prayer

TEXT: ACTS 2:42, 3:1

They devoted themselves to the apostles' teaching and fellowship, to the breaking of bread and the prayers. . . . One day Peter and John were going up to the temple at the hour of prayer, at three o'clock in the afternoon.

Formed on the day of Pentecost in Acts 2, this new community of Jesus followers "devoted themselves to the apostles' teaching and fellowship, to the breaking of bread and the prayers" (Acts 2:42). Teaching, eating, and shared resources formed this new community, and prayer also formed them.

Luke is specific. He identifies this component as "the prayers." Most likely, Luke is referring to the daily habit of Jewish believers praying in the temple at specified hours. For example, we know Peter and John regularly went up to the temple "at the hour of prayer," which was three o'clock in the afternoon (Acts 3:1). The early community worshiped in the temple daily, and they participated in those daily temple prayers. They continued the prayer practices of their Jewish heritage, including the singing or reciting of the psalms (which was part of Israel's prayer life).

Moreover, they embraced the prayer life of their Messiah. As the Gospel of Luke tells us, Jesus had a regular habit of prayer. He prayed at his baptism (Luke 3:21) and transfiguration (Luke 9:28). He prayed in the temple with other Jewish believers (Luke 19:46) and with his disciples (Luke 11:1–2), and he prayed alone (Luke 5:16, 6:12, 9:18). Disciples of Jesus, like their Messiah, are praying people.

This is what we see throughout the Book of Acts as renewed Israel continues to pray to God. When threatened by the ruling powers in Jerusalem, the church gathered to pray that the good news of the kingdom might have a hearing in their city (Acts 4:31). When threatened by the ruling powers, the church gathered to pray for the release of Peter from imprisonment (Acts 12:5). The apostles engaged not only in the ministry of the word but also prayer (Acts 6:4). When they sent people to serve in other places in the world, they prayed over them (Acts 13:3), and when they appointed leaders in various congregations, they prayed over them (Acts 14:23). They prayed when in prison (Acts 16:25), they prayed for healing (Acts 28:8), and they prayed in the temple (Acts 22:17).

Prayer was personal, and it was communal. Individuals sought God in prayer, and the community prayed together. It was bold, habitual, and diverse in its circumstances and significance.

Sometimes, it seems, the church is more focused on teaching than prayer, even more focused on the breaking of bread than prayer. However, it appears from the Book of Acts that prayer has a persistent presence that exceeds even teaching, fellowship, and the breaking of bread. Prayer, we might say, is the glue that held the church together through its many trials, persecutions, and growth spurts. Through prayer, the church depended upon God's work among them and for them. Through prayer, the church cast a vision for the future and trusted God with that future. We might say that the church cocreated the future with God through prayer, and that is the power of prayer itself.

QUESTION: In your experience, are disciples of Jesus devoted to prayer?

PRAYER: *Teach us, O God, to pray more fervently, more frequently, and more earnestly.*

THE FORMATION OF COMMUNITY

Leadership

TEXT: EPHESIANS 4:7–8, 11–12

But each of us was given grace according to the measure of Christ's gift.
Therefore it is said,
"When he ascended on high he made captivity itself a captive;
he gave gifts to his people." . . .
The gifts he gave were that some would be apostles, some prophets, some evangelists, some pastors and teachers, to equip the saints for the work of ministry, for building up the body of Christ.

When God liberated Israel from Egypt, God sent Moses, Aaron, and Miriam (Mic. 6:4) to lead them. When Jesus ascended to the right hand of God, he gave leadership gifts to renewed Israel.

God gifted people as apostles, prophets, evangelists, and pastors and teachers (a single group). Each leads in different ways, though the precise differentiation is undefined. Whatever one might say about their distinct roles, together, they form a leadership team within the body of Christ with both local and universal aspects.

While there are various ways to think about each of these roles, the body of Christ needs missionaries (i.e., people sent to plant churches), prophets (i.e., people who speak truth to power), evangelists (i.e., people who proclaim the good news of Jesus), and shepherds/teachers (i.e., people who guide local congregations). Whether local or universal, they are gifted to serve the church, the body of Christ. They provide servant leadership by living lives worthy of the gospel, ministering to the body of Christ, and heralding the word of life among the nations.

Leaders, however, have a specific work in relation to church. Their purpose is to equip the saints for ministry. They do not lead in order to consume the resources of the church or to promote their own prestige and power. On the contrary, they lead in order to raise up others to participate in the ministry of Christ with them. They lead in order to include others rather than lord over them. If leaders do not equip others, they abuse their gifts by exhausting them in their own interests rather than in the interest of others.

Leaders invite others to fully participate in the ministry of Jesus. The saints, or members of the body of Christ, are also gifted to participate, and leaders must devote themselves to fully equipping them. Everyone has a gift (Rom. 12:3–8), and everyone has a role in the community of faith (1 Cor. 12:4–11). Without everyone's participation, the church cannot fully become what God intends it to be, where every member utilizes their gifts for the growth and maturation of the body.

This is the purpose of both leadership and member participation. Leaders equip and members serve so the body may grow up into the full stature of Christ. Each part of the body works to promote the maturation of the whole in love. In this way, the body grows up in every way into the head, who is Jesus. As the head of the church, Jesus is the source of its life and love, and when the body matures, it becomes like Jesus in every way.

This is the work to which leaders and members are called—to grow up and become like Jesus. And this means the body joins Jesus in his ministry to serve the world and bless the nations.

QUESTION: What is the relationship between leaders and members, and what should characterize this relationship?

PRAYER: *God, give us godly leaders who faithful equip and love your people for the sake of your mission in the world.*

MISSIONAL MANDATE
Fill the Earth

TEXT: ACTS 2:47B, 6:7, 12:24

And day by day the Lord added to their number those who were being saved. . . . The word of God continued to spread; the number of the disciples increased greatly in Jerusalem, and a great many of the priests became obedient to the faith. . . . But the word of God continued to advance and gain adherents.

In the beginning of the theodrama, God created humanity as God's image upon the Earth and blessed them with a vocation. God called humanity to partner with God in the filling, cocreating, and shepherding of the creation. That we are the image of God is our identity, and the task God has given us is our vocation. We are both God's image and God's partners.

When God chose Israel as the firstborn among the nations, God invested this same identity and vocation in their life. The people of Israel were God's children or image, and they were tasked with filling the land God had given them, creating a just and compassionate society as a light to the nations, and caring for the land God had given them.

When God poured out the Holy Spirit on Pentecost, God renewed Israel, and this included Israel's mission. The new community would extend this human vocation through its commitment to the reign of God in the world through the Lord Jesus, Israel's Messiah. Renewed Israel was to fill the Earth with the glory of God, create just and compassionate communities as lights among the nations, and care for the Earth. While the human vocation was the vocation of renewed Israel, that vocation was also enlarged as renewed Israel represented the reign of the Messiah and served the goals of the Messiah for the creation.

The first task of the kingdom of God is to fill the Earth. The original commission in Genesis 1 is to "be fruitful and multiply and fill the earth" (Gen. 1:22). The Book of Acts applies this same language to the community of Jesus. For example, Acts 6 uses the same words from the Greek translation of Genesis 1. In Acts 6:1, "the disciples were increasing [or, multiplying] in number" as the Word of God was fruitful and continued to grow and spread. Further, Acts 12:24 says that the Word of God continued to advance and gain disciples of Jesus. Or, translated another way, the church continued to grow and multiply. The church experienced the blessing of God's work so that it became fruitful and multiplied.

Just as humanity was fruitful and multiplied in the beginning, and just as Israel was fruitful and multiplied in Egypt and in Canaan, the church was fruitful and multiplied in Jerusalem, in Judea, and to the ends of the Earth. The Jesus community is a discipling movement. The disciples grew and multiplied by making disciples—by inviting others into the kingdom of God through faith in God's Messiah. The early church followed Jesus, who himself made disciples and called his disciples to make disciples by baptizing them into the name of the triune God and teaching them to follow Jesus in everything.

In this way, the disciples of Jesus will fill the Earth with the glory of God. Just as divine image bearers were to fill the Earth with other image bearers, disciples of Jesus are to fill the Earth with other disciples of Jesus.

This was part of Paul's excitement when he wrote to the Colossians. He gave thanks to God that just as the gospel "is bearing fruit and growing in the whole world, so it has been bearing fruit among" them from the first day they heard the story of God's kingdom (Col. 1:6).

The goal of God is that Jesus himself will "fill all things" (Eph. 4:10). Part of the process by which Jesus fills the Earth is by disciples making disciples. This is our kingdom vocation.

QUESTION: What does it mean for the church to "be fruitful and multiply" and thus embrace the creation mandate as well as fulfill the mission of Israel?

PRAYER: *Place in our hearts the desire to make disciples and fill the Earth with your glory, O God.*

MISSIONAL MANDATE

Subdue the Powers

TEXT: ACTS 4:23–31

After they were released, they went to their friends and reported what the chief priests and the elders had said to them. When they heard it, they raised their voices together to God and said, "Sovereign Lord, who made the heaven and the earth, the sea, and everything in them, it is you who said by the Holy Spirit through our ancestor David, your servant:

'Why did the Gentiles rage,
and the peoples imagine vain things?
The kings of the earth took their stand,
and the rulers have gathered together
against the Lord and against his Messiah.'

For in this city, in fact, both Herod and Pontius Pilate, with the Gentiles and the peoples of Israel, gathered together against your holy servant Jesus, whom you anointed, to do whatever your hand and your plan had predestined to take place. And now, Lord, look at their threats, and grant to your servants to speak your word with all boldness, while you stretch out your hand to heal, and signs and wonders are performed through the name of your holy servant Jesus." When they had prayed, the place in which they were gathered together was shaken; and they were all filled with the Holy Spirit and spoke the word of God with boldness.

In the beginning, God created humanity as God's image to partner in the filling, cocreating, and shepherding of the creation, and then

God chose Israel as the firstborn among the nations to continue that mission and become a light to the nations. At Pentecost, God renewed Israel through the outpouring of the Holy Spirit and called this new Jesus community to fill the Earth with the glory of God, create just and compassionate communities as lights among the nations, and care for the Earth.

The first vocation is to fill the Earth, and disciples of Jesus fill the Earth by making disciples and mirroring the glory of God in their lives.

The second vocation is, according to Genesis 1:28, to subdue the Earth. But how do disciples of Jesus subdue the Earth? In Genesis, this means to subdue the remaining chaos within the creation and to cocreate with God in a way that brings order to the chaos that remains. We told that story in Day Seven. For example, software developers bring order to chaotic data so human beings have a greater opportunity to fully flourish as images of God. My TurboTax software program certainly helps me flourish during tax season, as it removes my anxiety, orders my financial chaos, and decreases my time investment.

But how does this vocation to subdue the Earth show up within the kingdom of Jesus? How do disciples of Jesus subdue the earth? Just as the kingdom vocation of filling the Earth was more than populating it, but also forming disciples in the image of Jesus, subduing the Earth is more than creating order out of chaos in terms of the natural world, but confronting, subverting, and redeeming the chaotic disorder that presently rules the world.

Jesus called Satan the "ruler" of this world who wields the principalities and powers to oppose the kingdom of our Lord Jesus (John 12:31; 14:30; 16:11). These principalities and powers come in many forms, including empires who oppress others, indwelling sin that enslaves us like an overwhelming addiction, and spiritual forces that array themselves against Jesus. The church, just as Jesus did in his ministry, confronts these powers, speaks truth to them, and subverts the powers by its obedience to the kingdom of God.

The Book of Acts records this vocation. When Peter and John were brought before the ruling Jewish council, they spoke truth to that power and declared they would obey God rather than any human authority. When Paul encountered evil spirits in Ephesus, he released the woman oppressed by their bondage, and the disciples confessed, disclosed their practices, and burned their books of sorcery (Acts 19:18–20). When Paul was brought before Felix, the Roman governor, he talked about "righteousness, self-control, and the judgment to come" (Acts 24:25 NIV).

Jesus is our example for how to subdue these powers. He did not draw the sword in violence and violently compel people into the kingdom of God. Quite the opposite. Through suffering love and compassion, Jesus undercut the powers through obedience to the will of God, an obedience that took him to a cross. Jesus overcame the powers through healing, reconciling, and forgiving, even as he exposed the darkness that was in the world. The apostles spoke the truth and confronted the powers about their evil actions, but they did not take those powers into their own hands. We are called to follow Jesus and unseat the powers through cups of cold water given to our enemies rather than through violence.

Subduing the Earth is the vocation with which God has tasked humanity—to bring order out of chaos—and this vocation is part of the reign of Jesus. Disciples of Jesus not only make disciples; they also confront and subvert the principalities and powers by their witness to the kingdom of God and by their obedience to King Jesus. Disciples of Jesus subvert and subdue the powers when they become like Jesus their king.

QUESTION: How might we fulfill the mission to subdue the powers in our context, and what does that look like?

PRAYER: *Deliver us, O Lord, from the evil one, and empower us to defeat the powers that oppress us and enslave the world.*

MISSIONAL MANDATE

Shepherd the Creation

TEXT: REVELATION 5:9–13

They sing a new song:
"You are worthy to take the scroll
and to open its seals,
for you were slaughtered and by your blood you ransomed for God
saints from every tribe and language and people and nation;
you have made them to be a kingdom and priests serving our God,
and they will reign on earth."
Then I looked, and I heard the voice of many angels surrounding the throne and the living creatures and the elders; they numbered myriads of myriads and thousands of thousands, singing with full voice,
"Worthy is the Lamb that was slaughtered
to receive power and wealth and wisdom and might
and honor and glory and blessing!"
Then I heard every creature in heaven and on earth and under the earth and in the sea, and all that is in them, singing,
"To the one seated on the throne and to the Lamb
be blessing and honor and glory and might
forever and ever!"

Just as God created humanity as partners in filling, cocreating, and shepherding the creation, and then invested Israel with the responsibility to continue this mission, on Pentecost, God inaugurated a new community through Jesus to fill the Earth with the glory of God, create just and compassionate communities as lights among the nations, and care for the Earth.

The first vocation is to fill the Earth, and disciples of Jesus fill the Earth by making disciples and mirroring the glory of God in their lives.

The second vocation is to subdue the Earth by creating order out of chaos, and disciples of Jesus embrace this vocation by subverting and opposing the principalities and powers that presently rule the creation.

The third vocation, according to Genesis 1:28, is to rule or shepherd the creation, which God loves and will one day liberate from its bondage to decay.

When the human vocation was described earlier in Day Eight, it was noted that ruling the Earth was not a function of cruel tyranny but of compassionate shepherding. We rule the Earth like shepherds caring for their flocks. This is our human vocation, and it is also the vocation of disciples of Jesus because they serve the Lord of creation, Jesus the Messiah.

Our task as human beings has not changed; we are still blessed by God to shepherd the creation. And renewed Israel, the kingdom of our Lord Jesus the Messiah, takes up this task in the midst of environmental chaos and destruction.

When the Word of God became flesh, God affirmed the goodness of creation. God became part of the creation through the Virgin Mary. As Jesus ministered within Israel, he healed the sick, restored sight to the blind, and raised the dead, and in this way, Jesus affirmed God's intent to heal the creation itself. When Jesus died, God raised him from the dead and gave him an immortal material body as the firstborn of the new creation, the new heaven and new Earth.

Enthroned alongside God, Jesus—along with the one seated on the throne—received the praise of "every creature in heaven and on earth and under the earth and in the sea, and all that is in them" (Rev. 5:13). All creation praises God and Jesus, and this creation exists by their will.

Our vocation, as disciples of Jesus, is to partner with God in caring for the creation. We protect the air and water of the Earth, preserve space for the animals, and care for rather than destroy the environment.

We reign with Christ over the cosmos. We are corulers, and our rule is a benevolent one, not a destructive one. When God finally redeems the creation and the kingdoms of this world become the kingdom of God's Messiah, God will, as Revelation 11:18 says, destroy "those who destroy the earth."

As co-regents with Jesus the Messiah, we share responsibility for the Earth. It is both our human and kingdom vocation. As a result, let us act responsibly toward the environment, and, at the very least, let us plant a tree, plant a garden, or care for animals.

QUESTION: Is the original mandate in creation to shepherd the creation still part of the mission of the disciples of Jesus? Why or why not?

PRAYER: *We love your creation, O Lord, because you are the maker of heaven and Earth!*

LIFE IN THE SPIRIT
Communion with God

TEXT: 2 CORINTHIANS 13:13

The grace of the Lord Jesus Christ, the love of God, and the communion of the Holy Spirit be with all of you.

Disciples of Jesus, like their Messiah, have been anointed with the Holy Spirit. Disciples of Jesus walk by the Spirit, live by the Spirit, and are led by the Spirit. The Spirit is the air we breathe and the one who empowers us. Ours is a life in the Spirit.

But what do we mean when we say that disciples of Jesus live in the Spirit? What does that look like, and how do we embody that in our lives and ministries?

For purposes of brevity, we may say that the theodrama emphasizes three dimensions of this life in the Spirit: (1) communion, (2) transformation, and (3) giftedness. We will address communion here and the other two over the next two days.

The Spirit is the one by whom we commune with the triune God. God dwells among us through the Spirit. Just as God was personally present in Israel through the temple and in the incarnation through Jesus, so God is personally present in the Jesus community through the indwelling Holy Spirit. We are the temple of God. The Spirit of God dwells among us and in us as a down payment for our future dwelling with the triune God in the new heaven and the new Earth.

Through the Spirit, we commune with and experience the person of God. The Spirit is the personal, existential connection between God and humanity. The personal indwelling of the Spirit is the experience of God in our hearts whereby we cry, "Abba." God and Christ come to dwell in us through the presence of the Spirit. The Spirit's foundational function is to mediate communion between God and us. Our communion with God is the "communion of the Holy Spirit" (2 Cor. 13:13).

The indwelling presence of the Spirit, which is the fulfillment of God's presence in the temple in Israel and anticipates the fullness of divine presence in the new heaven and new Earth, is how we now live in fellowship with God. We were washed in the Spirit (1 Cor. 6:11). We worship in the Spirit (Phil. 3:3). We pray in the Spirit (Eph. 6:18). We are "in the Spirit, since the Spirit of God dwells" in us (Rom. 8:9). The Spirit is the air we breathe, and our every breath is communion with God.

This communion is not merely vertical; it is also horizontal. We commune with each other by what we share in the Spirit (Phil 2:1). We love each other in the Spirit (Col. 1:8). Because we have all been baptized in the Spirit and have drunk of the same Spirit, we are one body. Ethnic, economic, and gender barriers are transcended in the body of Christ (1 Cor. 12:13; Gal. 3:28).

We see the Spirit among us when we enjoy the sweet fellowship of others, experience the peace and joy of the Spirit in communion with God, and encounter God in the assembly of God's people as we worship in the Spirit. We must not secularize these moments as if they are produced by our own internal powers. Instead, we relish them and delight in them because we know, by God's promise, that the Spirit is present to generate them. They are moments where heaven and Earth meet in the Spirit.

QUESTION: How is the Holy Spirit the means of communion between God and humanity, and what does that look like?

PRAYER: *Fill us, O God, with your Holy Spirit that we might know you more deeply and experience your love more profoundly.*

LIFE IN THE SPIRIT

Transformation

TEXT: 2 CORINTHIANS 3:17–18

Now the Lord is the Spirit, and where the Spirit of the Lord is, there is freedom. And all of us, with unveiled faces, seeing the glory of the Lord as though reflected in a mirror, are being transformed into the same image from one degree of glory to another; for this comes from the Lord, the Spirit.

Disciples of Jesus live in the Spirit. The theodrama emphasizes three dimensions of this life in the Spirit: (1) communion, (2) transformation, and (3) giftedness.

First, as noted in the previous day, the Spirit is the one by whom we commune with the triune God.

Second, we turn our attention to the work of the Spirit in transformation. Through this communion, the Holy Spirit's powerful presence transforms us into the image of Christ. The Spirit indwells us to empower, strengthen, and sanctify us. The Spirit is no passive presence but an active one. The Spirit bears the fruit of love, peace, and joy in our lives; it comforts us in our inner person; it empowers forgiveness and release from resentment; and it enables our transformation. The Spirit dwells within us so that we might live in the Spirit. Salvation includes transformation. Because we are children of God, God sends the Holy Spirit into our hearts, and we experience the intimacy of divine communion. But this is not the endgame; it is not God's goal. This intimacy includes a shared life, and it transforms us. We are increasingly, by the Spirit, transformed (metamorphized) into the image of Christ from "one degree of glory to another" (2 Cor. 3:18).

God's holy presence bears fruit. Paul called this the "fruit of the Spirit" (Gal. 5:22). A person who "lives by the Spirit" (Gal. 5:16, 25) will manifest a life of love, joy, peace, kindness, generosity, faithfulness, gentleness, and self-control. The Spirit leads us into a such a life by renewing our hearts, empowering our souls, and moving our wills.

The Spirit's presence is a necessary first step for such a life, and without that presence, our life cannot be transformed into the image of Jesus, who himself was led and empowered by the Spirit. The reality of this presence is evidenced in a holy life, as we are sanctified "by the Spirit" (2 Thess. 2:13).

We see the Spirit when we are patient with the stubborn, when we are kind to the ungrateful, when we are at peace in the midst of the storm, when we are generous with the poor, and when we are gentle with those whom with we disagree. We must not secularize these moments as if they are personal self-actualizations. Instead, we give thanks that the Spirit is at work in our lives. We credit the Spirit rather than our programs, our willpower, or our own goodness. God, by the Spirit, forms us into the image of Christ, and that is the glory and goal God has in store for us.

QUESTION: What is transformation, and how is the Spirit involved in our transformation?

PRAYER: *Transform us, O God, into the image of your Messiah!*

LIFE IN THE SPIRIT
Gifts

TEXT: 1 CORINTHIANS 12:4–7

Now there are varieties of gifts, but the same Spirit; and there are varieties of services, but the same Lord; and there are varieties of activities, but it is the same God who activates all of them in everyone. To each is given the manifestation of the Spirit for the common good.

Disciples of Jesus live in the Spirit. The theodrama emphasizes three dimensions of this life in the Spirit: (1) communion, (2) transformation, and (3) giftedness.

First, as previously discussed, the Spirit is the one by whom we commune with the triune God. Second, the Spirit is the one by whom God transforms us into the image of Christ. Last, we turn our attention to the gifts the Holy Spirit distributes within the body of Christ.

The Spirit distributes the gifts of God. These gifts range from gifts of mercy, teaching, leadership, and generosity (Rom. 12:3–8) to wisdom, knowledge, healings, miracles, prophesy, and tongues (1 Cor. 12:8–10). These lists are not exhaustive but are illustrative of God's work within the community of faith for the sake of the body and the world. The same Spirit disperses a diversity of gifts (1 Cor. 12:11).

The Spirit gifts each of us to serve, empowering us for ministry and life in the world. The Spirit equips for the "common good"—for communities of faith, for human society, and for creation. We seek these gifts through prayer, discipleship, and mentoring relationships.

God gives the Spirit as a communing and transforming presence in order to include us in the holy family of God. And there is more. The Holy Spirit gifts us so we might participate in the mission of the triune God.

"Through the Spirit," Paul wrote, God gives the body of Christ the capacity to serve each other and the world. These "manifestations of the Spirit" are for the "common good," and the gifts are "activated" and distributed by the Spirit of God (1 Cor. 12:7–8, 11).

It is important, however, to note that presence comes first, then transformation, and, finally, giftedness. We might think of this as a spiral of activity in which there is reciprocity but also movement toward a goal. God dwells in order to commune. That communion transforms us, and, as people in the process of transformation, God gifts us so we might participate in the mission of God. The gifts are best used by transformed people. Giftedness without love is useless; more than useless, it is detrimental. Transformation must shape the use of the Spirit's gifts.

The gifts of the Spirit refer to whatever capacity we have to participate in the mission of God. Whatever talent we use to further the mission of God—whether it is software development, musical ability, or environmental passion—they are the gifts of God. Too often we talk about talents as if they are natural dispositions independent of God's work among us. One of the reasons we feel so distant from the Holy Spirit is because we secularize our gifts. We minimize the Spirit's role. Giftedness, inclusive of talents, is a manifestation of the Spirit.

We see the Spirit when transformed people (or, better, people in the process of transformation) use their gifts to further the mission of God, which is the transformation of the whole world. We see the Spirit when an environmental biologist cares for the creation, when a nurse compassionately cares for the sick, when a debt mediator reconciles a creditor and a debtor, and when an actor embodies the gospel in a drama (even if the drama never mentions God at all). We see the Spirit's gifts in action when brokenness is healed.

The Spirit gifts us not for our own glory but for the glory of God as the mission of God is furthered in the world.

QUESTION: What are your gifts, and how have you used them for the sake of the body of Christ as well as for the world?

PRAYER: *Gift us, O God, by your Spirit that we might pursue your mission in the world.*

ACT FIVE

NEW CREATION

ALREADY, BUT NOT YET

TEXT: ROMANS 8:18–23

I consider that the sufferings of this present time are not worth comparing with the glory about to be revealed to us. For the creation waits with eager longing for the revealing of the children of God; for the creation was subjected to futility, not of its own will but by the will of the one who subjected it, in hope that the creation itself will be set free from its bondage to decay and will obtain the freedom of the glory of the children of God. We know that the whole creation has been groaning in labor pains until now; and not only the creation, but we ourselves, who have the first fruits of the Spirit, groan inwardly while we wait for adoption, the redemption of our bodies.

For disciples of Jesus, living in the present world is shaped by three horizons. First, we (along with everyone else) recognize that the present creation is filled with violence and suffering; it is filled with evil. The human condition is far from ideal, as racism, homophobia, sexism, murder, and injustice appear at every turn. Moreover, tsunamis, earthquakes, tornadoes, and hurricanes leave a path of destruction in their wake. As the apostle Paul put it, the creation has been subjected to futility or frustration. The creation has not yielded its full promise but lives in bondage given over to decay. Consequently, even the creation itself, along with all humanity, groans for liberation; it groans for redemption.

At the same time, though groaning with creation, disciples of Jesus also experience joy and hope because new creation has already begun, and even now, we enjoy the fruit of God's redemptive work. For example, we already experience redemption through the presence of the indwelling Holy Spirit, who is the first fruit of a coming harvest. By the presence of the Spirit, we already participate in the new creation. The Holy Spirit knows our hearts, searches them, and intercedes for us. The Holy Spirit groans with us and also secures our hearts through the hope of redemption and liberation. While we groan over the brokenness and violence that is still part of the present creation, we may also know peace, joy, and hope by the presence of the Spirit in our hearts.

We groan because we have not yet fully experienced the promise of a new creation. At present, the creation groans in its bondage, and we groan over the evil in the world, as well as our own suffering. Nevertheless, we are rescued through this groaning by hope, which is poured into our hearts by the power of the Holy Spirit. Our hope is the future redemption of our bodies in the resurrection, as well as the future liberation of creation. We hope for the fullness of new creation when God will renew the present creation and rid it of its evils, sufferings, and chaos. While we have not yet experienced this future, it is our hope. Because God has raised Jesus from the dead and poured the Spirit into our hearts, we wait in hopeful expectation for that future.

We wait. That is the difficult part. Waiting involves endurance, because our hopes and dreams are not immediately realized. Sometimes it seems they are mere illusions, the product of self-deception and wishful thinking. Waiting is a process of endurance drawn from the witness of the Spirit in our hearts, who orients us to the future God is preparing for us. But waiting is hard.

This is one reason the disciples of Jesus live under three horizons. On one hand, we acknowledge the reality of the present evil age, and we suffer because of it. Yet, on the other hand, we already know the joy of the presence of the Holy Spirit in our hearts, which enables our endurance. But—and this is the third horizon—we do not yet fully experience what God has in store for us. We live between the times. We name the evil of the present age, while we, at the same time, know the joy of the Spirit as we await the future.

QUESTION: In what ways do you experience life "in between" times?

PRAYER: *Hear our groans, O Lord, and fill us with hope.*

PERFECTED THROUGH SUFFERING

TEXT: HEBREWS 5:8–10

Although he was a Son, he learned obedience through what he suffered; and having been made perfect, he became the source of eternal salvation for all who obey him, having been designated by God a high priest according to the order of Melchizedek.

Why does God permit suffering in God's good creation? Everyone from the small child to the career philosopher and theologian has asked this question. But I have an answer, which, for me, is the only honest answer. I don't know. I simply don't know. Whatever reasons God may have for permitting evil and suffering, I certainly don't know them, and because of this, it is difficult for me to recognize such reasons. Though the story of God does not leave us totally clueless, even if I had some sense of the depth of God's reasons, I would never understand them. My intelligence is too shallow, my perspective is too limited, and my heart is too self-interested to fully understand God's rationale. In other words, my brain is too small to accommodate the fullness of God's wisdom.

At the same time, the theodrama, the story of God, is not silent about suffering. It provides the most astounding response to suffering the world has ever heard. It is the story of Jesus.

God became a human being; God became flesh. As a human being, subject to the pains and struggles of the present creation because of that flesh, God suffered alongside us. God suffered with us. Prior to this incarnation, God had never experienced hunger, thirst, or death. God had never experienced the temptations of the flesh. God became one of us so God might know us from the inside out as one who has walked in our shoes and fully experienced the human condition, particularly our suffering.

But that is only the beginning. The preacher in Hebrews describes this reality with shocking language. Jesus, the incarnate God, was *perfected* through suffering (Heb. 2:10, 5:8–10). But what does that mean?

In part, it refers to the process of spiritual formation that matures our character through the trials of life. Jesus certainly experienced this in the wilderness as well as throughout his life. He grew in wisdom, and he learned obedience by the things from which he suffered. In this way, God uses suffering to bear the fruit of righteousness in the lives of the disciples of Jesus (Heb. 12:11).

But I think we can say more. Jesus, as God incarnate, followed us into our suffering not only to share in it but also to lead us out of it. He came to defeat it, overcome it, and liberate us from it. He followed us into death and pursued us into the grave. But Jesus suffered in order to create a path out of suffering so he might bring others to glory with him. He freed the enslaved and forged a path through suffering into glory. He was perfected through suffering so he might perfect us.

In this way, Jesus not only shares our suffering, but we also share his. When we suffer, we suffer with Jesus just as he suffered for us. When we follow Jesus into his ministry, our discipleship shares in the affliction of Jesus, and by this we know the fellowship of his suffering. And if we know the fellowship of his suffering, we will also know the power of his resurrection—not just in the future but even in the present (Phil. 3:10). We know that if we suffer with him, just as he suffered with us, we will also be glorified with him, just as he was glorified in his resurrection and exaltation (Rom. 8:17).

QUESTION: What does God's response to suffering in Jesus tell us about suffering?

PRAYER: *Thank you, Lord, for your love; though you were rich, you became poor for our sake.*

LIFE IN THE SPIRIT
Lament

TEXT: ROMANS 8:22–27

We know that the whole creation has been groaning in labor pains until now; and not only the creation, but we ourselves, who have the first fruits of the Spirit, groan inwardly while we wait for adoption, the redemption of our bodies. For in hope we were saved. Now hope that is seen is not hope. For who hopes for what is seen? But if we hope for what we do not see, we wait for it with patience.

Likewise the Spirit helps us in our weakness; for we do not know how to pray as we ought, but that very Spirit intercedes with sighs too deep for words. And God, who searches the heart, knows what is the mind of the Spirit, because the Spirit intercedes for the saints according to the will of God.

Life in the Spirit is always filled with joy, but it is also always filled with lament.

That sounds strange, doesn't it? How can it be both? It is both because we live in between times. We rejoice because we already know God's salvation, and at the same time, we groan over the sufferings of this present world. We are always groaning and rejoicing because we live in this moment when, though new creation has already begun, it has not yet been fully realized.

Some think that Christians should only rejoice, no matter what their circumstances. They find no place for lament as people who live in the Spirit. While there is always a place for gratitude in our lives, even when we are suffering, there is also space for lament as well. Though, for example, Paul was filled with hope and joy, he also groaned. Even though we have the first fruits of the Spirit, we still groan while we wait for the fullness of new creation (Rom. 8:23).

Lament, grief, and protest have their rightful place in hearts filled with the Spirit of God. Jesus himself lamented on the cross, wept at the grave of a friend, and protested unjust economics at the temple. Indeed, we might say that the presence of the Spirit gives us voice in such laments, griefs, and protests.

It is because we are filled with the Spirit and enjoy the fruit of the Spirit in our lives that our voices are raised in lament. We groan over the suffering and evil in creation, and we raise our voices in petitioning God to end this suffering and rid the world of evil.

It is because we are filled with the Spirit and enjoy the fruit of the Spirit in our lives that we weep over death, violence, and injustice. At the graves of family and friends, we weep, but not as those who have no hope. We weep over the violence that fills the Earth, including in our schools and homes.

It is because we are filled with the Spirit and enjoy the fruit of the Spirit in our lives that we protest the injustice in the world. We protest against evil in all its forms, including racial, economic, and gender injustice. We raise our voices in complaint, and we ask God to do something about the injustices that surround us.

Life in the Spirit means that we groan, and our groanings take the form of lament, grief, and protest. We lament, in part, because the Spirit beckons us to a future when there is no suffering, death, and injustice. We grieve because the Spirit moves us to acknowledge the frustrations of a creation bound over to decay. We protest because the Spirit has instilled in us a hope and longing for the fullness of new creation.

When we lament, grieve, or protest, we join our voices with the voice of the Spirit, who also laments, grieves, and protests.

QUESTION: Why does lament often feel so unchristian to many disciples of Jesus?

PRAYER: *How long, O Lord, before you redeem your creation?*

LIFE IN THE SPIRIT
Waiting in Hope

TEXT: ROMANS 5:1–5

Therefore, since we are justified by faith, we have peace with God through our Lord Jesus Christ, through whom we have obtained access to this grace in which we stand; and we boast in our hope of sharing the glory of God. And not only that, but we also boast in our sufferings, knowing that suffering produces endurance, and endurance produces character, and character produces hope, and hope does not disappoint us, because God's love has been poured into our hearts through the Holy Spirit that has been given to us.

Life in the Spirit is always filled with joy, though it is also always filled with lament.

It is both because we live in between times. We rejoice because we already know God's salvation, and at the same time, we ache over the sufferings of this present world. We are always groaning and rejoicing because we live in this moment when, though new creation has already begun, it has not yet been fully realized.

This means we must wait. Waiting is precarious. It doesn't always feel safe. Indeed, it is perilous at times and often uncertain. Waiting is painful; it opens the door to fear. Waiting tests faith. Waiting demands endurance. Though we already experience God's salvation through the presence of the Holy Spirit, we wait with endurance for the full realization of our hope (Rom. 8:26).

While we wait, we often suffer. But this suffering, as strange as it may sound, is something in which we boast. Paul tells us that we boast not only "in our hope of sharing the glory of God," but that we also "boast in our sufferings" (Rom. 5:2–3).

It makes sense to boast in hope. Standing in the grace of God, we have peace with God because we have been declared right with God through Jesus the Messiah. Therefore, we have hope. But this hope has not yet been fully realized, and, consequently, we wait. As we wait, we suffer. And we boast in our sufferings.

Still, does it make sense to boast in suffering? Wherein does the boast lie? Is suffering meaningful? What is gained through suffering?

Paul boasted in suffering because he knew what it produced. We boast in suffering, Paul says, because we know it produces endurance. The word *endurance* refers to something that stands up under pressure. We are squeezed, pressed, and molded into something. Suffering is a crucible, a kind of pressure cooker. What is produced is something that has withstood the pressure and been formed by it.

We boast in suffering, Paul says, because we know that endurance produces character. This is what pressure produces. The Greek word for *character* refers to a tested character or, as one older translation puts it, "approvedness" (Rom. 5:4 ASV). Endurance produces an approved character, one that has been tested and refined by process. Through suffering, we grow into something; we gain something. Suffering produces a tested and formed faith.

We boast in suffering, Paul says, because we know that character produces hope. At some point, we confess that the process of suffering has produced something worth the struggle: hope. It is out of the suffering that we learn to hope, and it is because we stand in the grace of God that we are able to hope. Suffering does not subvert our hope. Suffering produces hope, and hope does not disappoint us.

Hope, however, is not some kind of self-actualization as if we produce hope through our own efforts or right thinking. On the contrary, hope is something produced through suffering, because the Holy Spirit's presence pours the love of God into our hearts.

Suffering, then, produces hope because we know God's love through faith, and we experience the hope of the Holy Spirit in the process of endurance that forms our character. We hope because of what God does by pouring the Spirit into our hearts, and we experience that hope through the suffering we endure. In this way, we wait in hope.

QUESTION: Is it possible, in this moment or in relation to the past, to boast in your suffering?

PRAYER: *Pour your love into our hearts, O God, that we might see what suffering has produced in our lives through your Spirit and by your mercy.*

THE RESURRECTION OF JESUS

TEXT: 1 CORINTHIANS 15:21–28

For since death came through a human being, the resurrection of the dead has also come through a human being; for as all die in Adam, so all will be made alive in Christ. But each in his own order: Christ the first fruits, then at his coming those who belong to Christ. Then comes the end, when he hands over the kingdom to God the Father, after he has destroyed every ruler and every authority and power. For he must reign until he has put all his enemies under his feet. The last enemy to be destroyed is death. For "God has put all things in subjection under his feet." But when it says, "All things are put in subjection," it is plain that this does not include the one who put all things in subjection under him. When all things are subjected to him, then the Son himself will also be subjected to the one who put all things in subjection under him, so that God may be all in all.

Death is an enemy.

On occasion, death can be a relative good. When quality of life, for example, is significantly diminished and there is unbearable pain, we might think dying is better than living, but only in a relative sense. Life is better than death since God created us for life, not death.

But death, the enemy, reigns. We are powerless before it. We cannot control it. We have no authority over it. Death comes when it will. We may be able to delay it, but it still comes.

Indeed, death has a long history. Though shalom or peace once ruled the Garden of Eden, in which God delighted and where God rested, sin vandalized the goodness of creation, and death assumed its dictatorship. Death invaded Eden, and now chaos reigns through death. In Adam, Paul says, all die.

Without hope, death gives way to despair. But Jesus the Messiah is God's response to living east of Eden. Resurrection is God's answer to death. God does not intend for creation, including our bodies, to disappear into nothingness. God will raise our bodies from the dead that they might live in the renewed creation, the new heaven and new Earth.

God has a plan, and it is Jesus the Messiah. Jesus was not only human, but he is the new human through his resurrection. He is the first of a new humanity, one that will live forever in resurrected bodies on a renewed Earth. His resurrection promises a future for humanity. In Christ, Paul says, all are made alive.

Jesus is the first of a coming harvest. Jesus is the first fruit of that harvest; there is more to come. The resurrection of Jesus belongs to the future, even though it occurred in the past as a promise of the future.

The resurrection of Jesus is a preview of coming attractions. But this preview does not leave us wondering what the end of the drama is. Instead, in the resurrection of Jesus, we see death destroyed.

The resurrection of Jesus is the power of God that destroys all authority, power, and dominion. Death no longer reigns, but Jesus does. The empire no longer wields power, but the kingdom of God does. Satan no longer holds the keys of hades or death, but the living Christ does.

Death is the last enemy, and it will not last. Death will not win. This is what we celebrate every Sunday and on Easter. God has given us hope in this life, and through the resurrection, God will give us life after death.

God will not abandon God's people in the grave. Life wins. Death loses.

QUESTION: How does one grieve with hope in the light of the resurrection of Jesus?

PRAYER: *Thanks be to God for the immortal body of Jesus, our Lord!*

THE RESURRECTION OF HUMANITY

TEXT: 1 CORINTHIANS 15:50–57

What I am saying, brothers and sisters, is this: flesh and blood cannot inherit the kingdom of God, nor does the perishable inherit the imperishable. Listen, I will tell you a mystery! We will not all die, but we will all be changed, in a moment, in the twinkling of an eye, at the last trumpet. For the trumpet will sound, and the dead will be raised imperishable, and we will be changed. For this perishable body must put on imperishability, and this mortal body must put on immortality. When this perishable body puts on imperishability, and this mortal body puts on immortality, then the saying that is written will be fulfilled:

> *"Death has been swallowed up in victory."*
> *"Where, O death, is your victory?*
> *Where, O death, is your sting?"*

The sting of death is sin, and the power of sin is the law. But thanks be to God, who gives us the victory through our Lord Jesus Christ.

The hope of the Christian faith is the transformation of human life from its present bondage to sin and death into a new humanity, where the love of God is perfected in our souls and our bodies are equipped for living in the new heaven and new Earth. Our future glorification is a transformation into the likeness of Jesus the Messiah—the new human—in both body and soul. It is a passing from the present old way of living in God's good creation to a new way of living in God's new heaven and new Earth.

We are saved from death, and thus our bodies are resurrected and transformed. We are also saved from corruption, and our souls and hearts are fully transformed. Through our union with Christ, we become a recreated humanity as the image of God is renewed and glorified. This is our final state in glory when we are united with the glorified Christ, who is the new human, and we reign with him over creation in glorious, resurrected bodies.

This resurrected body is neither immaterial nor some kind of ethereal reality. Instead, it is material and spiritual. What I mean is that our bodies will have material substance. They will share in the materiality of the new heaven and new Earth but will be animated by the Holy Spirit rather than by "flesh and blood." The life of the immortal body is not sustained by food and blood as it is in the present Adamic world, but it is sustained by the life-giving Holy Spirit in the new creation conformed to the life of the new Adam, who is the Lord Jesus. The hope of the Christian faith is not an immortal soul, but an immortal body, which is a part of the new creation in the new heaven and new Earth. Our redemption—our salvation—includes the redemption of our bodies.

The soul—or whatever we call our inner selves—is perfected in the new heaven and new Earth. While the process of perfection began in the past and continues in the present, it is not complete until we fully participate in the life of Christ at our resurrection. Then we shall fully be as he is, though we do not know what that is like because we only now experience a foretaste of that future. We, like Jesus, will experience transfiguration in the new creation. We will be permanently transfigured into the fullness of God's likeness and will become a new humanity in both body and soul.

We will be saved in the new creation to image God in the new heaven and new Earth. We will be saved for eternal communion with God and to serve God as God's image bearers in the new temple, the new creation. God will restore our original dignity and function, and God will glorify us by reinstating our reign over the creation. In this way, with transformed bodies and souls, we will co-rule with God in the renewed cosmos.

QUESTION: What will we be like after our resurrection?

PRAYER: *Death, where is your victory? God, you have defeated it, defanged its power, and destroyed our fear. Thank you!*

THE RESURRECTION OF CREATION

TEXT: 2 PETER 3:11–13

Since all these things are to be dissolved in this way, what sort of persons ought you to be in leading lives of holiness and godliness, waiting for and hastening the coming of the day of God, because of which the heavens will be set ablaze and dissolved, and the elements will melt with fire? But, in accordance with his promise, we wait for new heavens and a new Earth, where righteousness is at home.

Though often neglected, salvation also includes the liberation of the cosmos from its bondage to decay and destruction. The whole cosmos groans, along with humanity, for relief from the frustration to which the world has been subjected. God saves the cosmos by renewing it, by ushering in a new or renewed heaven and Earth.

This hope is rooted in God's promise to Abraham. The land, which includes the whole cosmos, according to Romans 4:13, is the inheritance of Israel. Abraham is the heir of the cosmos. The creation now belongs to a descendant of Abraham, the son of David, the Son of God. As coheirs with Jesus, we, too, are heirs of the cosmos.

Based on this promise to Abraham, according to Peter, "we wait for the new heavens and a new earth, where righteousness is at home" (2 Pet. 3:13). God promised Abraham an inheritance, and that inheritance was a new heaven and a new earth. The Christian hope includes a new Earth.

Too often Christians have thought they must escape the creation and fly away in glory to some eternal celestial heaven as their final home. If we mean that we want to escape the present evil age or escape the decaying, destructive powers of death, then I understand that point. I, too, want to escape. God will dissolve all evil and destroy the powers that enslave creation. Yet, the biblical story is not ultimately about escape, but redemption.

God redeemed the body of Jesus by raising him from the dead and transforming his death-bound body into an immortal body. This is our hope as well. One day God will redeem our bodies by raising us from the dead and transforming our death-bound bodies into immortal bodies. This is also the hope of creation itself.

The creation groans to be "set free" or liberated from "its bondage to decay," and it hopes to share in the "freedom of the glory of the children of God" (Rom. 8:21). The resurrection of the creation is rooted in the resurrection of God's people, just as the resurrection of God's people is rooted in the resurrection of God's Messiah. The resurrection of Jesus, our own resurrection, and the resurrection of creation are inextricably tied together. The resurrection of Jesus has inaugurated the new creation, our resurrection is our participation in the new creation, and the creation itself becomes new because it is the dwelling place of the resurrected people of God with their resurrected Messiah.

In this way, the creation is like a mother about to give birth to something new (Rom. 8:22). The creation presently experiences something akin to labor pains as it groans in eager expectation for its liberation and transformation. The present creation will give birth to a new creation, just as our bodies will give birth to new bodies in the resurrection.

The Abrahamic promise was first given to ethnic Israel but, by faith and because of the Messiah, it includes the nations as well. Perhaps in the new heaven and new Earth the redeemed of ethnic Israel will dwell in Palestine—in the land between the rivers of Egypt and Babylon—and the rest of the Earth will belong to God's people among the nations as they again reign on the Earth with God. The kingdom of God will fill the Earth.

The Earth is the inheritance of God's people, as Jesus promised: The meek "will inherit the earth" (Matt. 5:5). One day, the reign of God will fill it from the east to the west, from the north to the south. The whole Earth, unlike its present condition, will be "Holy to the Lord" (Zech. 14:20).

QUESTION: Why is it important to think about the resurrection of creation as part of the theodrama?

PRAYER: *We yearn for the day, O God, when the whole Earth will be filled with your glory, and everything from its mountains and lakes to its pots and pans will be "holy to the Lord."*

DIVINE JUDGMENT

TEXT: REVELATION 20:11–15

Then I saw a great white throne and the one who sat on it; the earth and the heaven fled from his presence, and no place was found for them. And I saw the dead, great and small, standing before the throne, and books were opened. Also another book was opened, the book of life. And the dead were judged according to their works, as recorded in the books. And the sea gave up the dead that were in it, Death and Hades gave up the dead that were in them, and all were judged according to what they had done. Then Death and Hades were thrown into the lake of fire. This is the second death, the lake of fire; and anyone whose name was not found written in the book of life was thrown into the lake of fire.

As we read the story of God in the Bible, we see over and over again when God purposes to set things right, does set things right, and promises to ultimately set everything right. God will not let evil stand, God will not let evil go unchecked, and God will not let evil win.

When people filled the Earth with violence, God renewed the Earth with a flood. When Egypt would not let God's people go, it suffered divine judgment. When Israel did not care for its poor and shed innocent blood, God sent them into exile. When the Messiah came to the temple, he turned over its tables of injustice and exploitation. When the powers killed the Messiah, God judged the powers through the resurrection of the Messiah and set the world right through the exaltation of the Messiah to God's right hand.

God's vindication of the Messiah and its corresponding subversion of the powers is the revelation of God's final goal, which is: God will set things right.

This is the essence of divine judgment. God discerns between good and evil, God destroys evil, and God ensures the triumph of good. This is how the story of God has played out throughout the theodrama.

At the same time, God does not act as quickly or as thoroughly as we like. We want it over now, and we pray for the full reign of God in the world now. When we pray, "Your kingdom come, your will be done on earth as it is in heaven" (Matt. 6:10), we are praying for God's final discernment between good and evil, God's final destruction of evil, and God's final triumph over evil. We are praying that God will set things right. We are praying, "Come, Lord Jesus."

There will come a day, a judgment day, when the distinction between good and evil will become clear. We will see evil in all its stark reality, and we will reject it and acknowledge its opposition to the life of God. God will purge all evil from creation, and evil will be destroyed and eliminated from God's creation so there is no more curse, no more sea, and no more evil in God's new creation (Rev. 21:1–6, 22:3).

Judgment is that process by which God separates evil from good and separates the sheep from the goats. This separation not only identifies and clarifies the reality of evil, but it also refines and purifies people so that God's people are fully perfected in the love of God. Judgment, then, is the moment when evil is identified, humanity is examined, the Earth is purified by fire, the people of God are fully sanctified, and the people of God are invited into the new creation to live upon a new Earth where righteousness dwells.

It often seems like God does not care about evil because God permits it to exist in such quantity with such intensity. We sometimes doubt whether God is all that concerned about evil and the trauma it creates.

The story of God, however, assures us that God does care. God examines humanity, and God discerns the difference between good and evil. God will destroy evil, and good will triumph. We see this in the life, death, resurrection, and exaltation of Jesus. And that is our hope.

God will judge evil and exalt the good. So, we continue to pray, "Your Kingdom come, your will be done, on earth as it is in heaven."

QUESTION: What in our present world needs to be set right, and how does divine judgment address it?

PRAYER: *May your kingdom come, and may your will be done on Earth as it is in heaven.*

NEW HEAVEN AND NEW EARTH

Communal Life

TEXT: REVELATION 21:1–7

Then I saw a new heaven and a new Earth; for the first heaven and the first earth had passed away, and the sea was no more. And I saw the holy city, the new Jerusalem, coming down out of heaven from God, prepared as a bride adorned for her husband. And I heard a loud voice from the throne saying,

"See, the home of God is among mortals.
He will dwell with them as their God;
they will be his peoples,
and God himself will be with them;
he will wipe every tear from their eyes.
Death will be no more;
mourning and crying and pain will be no more,
for the first things have passed away."

And the one who was seated on the throne said, "See, I am making all things new." Also he said, "Write this, for these words are trustworthy and true." Then he said to me, "It is done! I am the Alpha and the Omega, the beginning and the end. To the thirsty I will give water as a gift from the spring of the water of life. Those who conquer will inherit these things, and I will be their God and they will be my children."

The goal of God for human life is transformation into the likeness of God and participation in the communal fellowship of the triune God. When humanity fully participates in the circle of God's loving fellowship, then the reign of God has fully arrived.

This does not entail a loss of finitude or creatureliness. When we are glorified in the new heaven and new Earth, our bodies will conform to the glorious body of the resurrected Lord. This does not mean we are saved from finitude. (Creatureliness is part of God's good creation.) Instead, we are invited, as finite creatures, to share in the divine fellowship of the triune God. We will not become omniscient or omnipotent because we will not participate in the divine essence. We will not become little gods, but we will become godlike—that is, full participants in divine love.

At the same time, our participation in divine love—because we experience such love as finite creatures—is an eternal journey into the heart of God as we move more deeply into our fellowship with the triune God throughout eternity. Every morning, God will be new to us because, as finite creatures, the infinite God will always have more to share with us, and we will experience that love more deeply. God is like a bottomless well from which we will drink. We will experience daily fillings of joy and satisfaction, but there is always more to drink. God will give us more, moment by moment, throughout eternity.

As community, we will grow more intimate with each other. The relationships we begin now will continue into glory. More than that, they will grow deeper, wider, and more inclusive. Our relationships will not remain static but will deepen and expand. We will know not only those with whom we have relationships now, but we will also initiate new relationships with people we have never known. The fullness of the kingdom of God as a community is an interactive web of relationships that provide opportunity for growth in the new heaven and new Earth.

Moreover, the glorified community is not a static accomplishment, as if we attain "perfection" and there is no more work, no more loving, no more growing, no more knowing, or no more connecting to be done. Rather, the fullness of the kingdom of God involves dynamic growth into the heart of God, as well as dynamic growth among the people of God. When God re-creates, just as God created in the beginning, the triune God will create a dynamic reality that invites the redeemed community to pursue growth, intimacy, fellowship, and relationship within the new creation.

The oneness of the people of God will emerge brightly upon the new Earth, and the unity of the body of Christ will be recognized as a gift of God's gracious work. But the oneness does not entail some kind of undifferentiated Stepford human beings as if we are clones or identical in every way. Instead, the oneness, like the oneness of the original creation, includes diversity and dynamism that reflect the reality of the loving God, who is both three and one.

The fullness of the kingdom, then, is a communal reality created in the image of God's triune fellowship. It is the experience of intimacy without fear, love without suspicion, and trust without doubt. It is love because God is love. There are no more barriers, ethnic bigotry, class wars, or alienation or marginalization. The kingdom of God will experience community in a way that images the community of God, and it will participate in the community of God.

QUESTION: How is communion a dynamic reality rather than a static one?

PRAYER: *May we find rest in you, O God, for eternity, and may we enjoy the communion of your divine love.*

A NEW GARDEN

Renewed Identity and Vocation

TEXT: REVELATION 22:1–5

Then the angel showed me the river of the water of life, bright as crystal, flowing from the throne of God and of the Lamb through the middle of the street of the city. On either side of the river is the tree of life with its twelve kinds of fruit, producing its fruit each month; and the leaves of the tree are for the healing of the nations. Nothing accursed will be found there any more. But the throne of God and of the Lamb will be in it, and his servants will worship him; they will see his face, and his name will be on their foreheads. And there will be no more night; they need no light of lamp or sun, for the Lord God will be their light, and they will reign forever and ever.

The new Earth has a new garden in a new city.

In Revelation 21:1, John sees a "new heaven and a new earth" where God's new Jerusalem descends from heaven to Earth. In other words, heaven comes down to Earth. At that moment, the whole Earth is filled with the glory of God.

There is no more chaos, which is represented by the absence of a sea. There is no more death, pain, or mourning because all of that has passed away and because everything has become new. As God says, "I am making all things new" (Rev. 21:5). The text does not say that God makes new things, but that God *will* make all things new. God renews what

God made in the beginning, which fulfills God's promise to Abraham, and God then invites the children of Abraham to "inherit these things" (Rev. 21:7).

When heaven comes to Earth, heaven and Earth become one. That union of heaven and Earth—the union of the dwelling of God with the dwelling of humanity within the creation—is the very moment when the glory of God will fill the Earth. Everything within it will be called holy, and the Earth will know the righteousness, justice, and peace of the fullness of the kingdom of God.

This was the hope of Israel. They yearned for a time of peace and justice, of righteousness and love. They hoped for a time when the wolf and the lamb would lie down together. They expected a time when all the nations would bow before their God and learn war no more. They trusted that God would reign fully on the Earth. These are the promises and prophecies that will be fulfilled when God renews the heavens and the Earth, coming to dwell with the heirs of the promise on the new Earth.

The new Earth has a new city, the new Jerusalem. This is the city where God dwells. There is no temple in this city because God fully dwells there. There is no night there because God is the light of the city. The whole Earth has become the temple of God, as the new Jerusalem fills the Earth.

This new city also has a new garden that gives life to God's people. The tree of life is there, and there is abundant provision for all peoples.

In this new city, with its new garden on a new Earth, the people of God serve God day and night. I don't know exactly what that means. In what ways will we serve God? Perhaps we will take up our original commission to reign with God over the creation, which means we will continue to develop and care for it.

Perhaps we might imagine that we continue to write new songs, create new art, make new history, build new buildings, and develop new relationships with people and diverse nations. Perhaps we will finally learn to enjoy the diversity of different cultures and peoples. To serve God is to continue in the ministry God gave humanity, to function as royal priests within creation. We will lead creation in the praise of God, and we will care for the creation and develop its potential even further.

Exactly what will that look like? I don't know, and I hesitate to speculate. But I am confident of this: It will be a grand adventure that exceeds all that we might imagine and more than anything for which we might ask. It will be a great adventure, and the story of God will continue and blossom into eternity.

QUESTION: What do you imagine life on the new Earth will be like, and how does it continue the journey we have begun on Earth at present?

PRAYER: *Praise God, who richly blesses us with good things!*

Also by John Mark Hicks

EMBRACING CREATION

God's Forgotten Mission

JOHN MARK HICKS, BOBBY VALENTINE, & MARK WILSON

ISBN 978-0-89112-336-1

The world around you isn't a playground or a mission field. It's more than that . . .

Embracing Creation tells the story of the relationship between God, humanity, and Creation. God calls humanity to preserve, develop, and love his good Creation, his cosmic temple. Recalling the original story of Creation, the authors retell the story of Israel, Jesus, and the Church in light of God's love for the cosmos. Through the resurrection of Jesus, God redeems humanity and Creation from the bondage of death.

Learn to embrace Creation—protecting the earth's resources, subduing its chaos, rejoicing in its gifts, and meditating on its splendor in worship. God created something good and intends to make it even better. The good Creation is not to be annihilated but made new for an eternal habitation of God with humanity.

"Everyone now knows about the deep seriousness of our environmental crisis. These authors make a vigorous, compelling response to that crisis with acute theological probes. They mobilize the entire witness of Scripture and make clear that the well-being of creation is no incidental matter to the gospel. That wellbeing, as they show, is a primary gift and intent of the creator and a primary human task. The good news pertains to all of creation, so the argument goes, or it is no good news at all."

—**WALTER BRUEGGEMANN,** Columbia Theological Seminary

1-877-816-4455 toll free
www.leafwoodpublishers.com